EDUCATORS
as Writers

PETER LANG
New York • Washington, D.C./Baltimore • Bern
Frankfurt am Main • Berlin • Brussels • Vienna • Oxford

EDUCATORS
as Writers

Publishing for Personal
and Professional Development

Carol Smallwood,
EDITOR

PETER LANG
New York • Washington, D.C./Baltimore • Bern
Frankfurt am Main • Berlin • Brussels • Vienna • Oxford

Library of Congress Cataloging-in-Publication Data

Educators as writers: publishing for personal and professional development /
Carol Smallwood, editor.
p. cm.
Includes bibliographical references.
1. Authorship—Vocational guidance.
I. Smallwood, Carol. II. Title.
PN147.E29   808'.02023—dc22   2006012715
ISBN 0-8204-8601-9

Bibliographic information published by **Die Deutsche Bibliothek**.
Die Deutsche Bibliothek lists this publication in the "Deutsche
Nationalbibliografie"; detailed bibliographic data is available
on the Internet at http://dnb.ddb.de/.

Cover design by Lisa Barfield

The paper in this book meets the guidelines for permanence and durability
of the Committee on Production Guidelines for Book Longevity
of the Council of Library Resources.

© 2006 Peter Lang Publishing, Inc., New York
29 Broadway, New York, NY 10006
www.peterlang.com

Printed in the United States of America

This collection is
dedicated to the
contributors for their
efforts in helping other
educators.

preface

Educators as Writers: Publishing for Personal and Professional Development is for elementary-college educators and students seeking insider tips from colleagues who've successfully published. The book came about after my own struggles in turning from writing reference books for over twenty years to fiction and poetry: I searched for tips on technique and marketing by those who'd "been there, done that" with a similar background.

The contributors (from Alaska to Arkansas, California to Maine) represent various stages in educational careers such as elementary teachers, college professors, school counselors, librarians, including a magazine and a book editor who've worked with educators.

Many educators indicate colleagues have asked them for tips on how to publish. I'm sure you've heard colleagues say, "I'm going to write a children's book some day," or "I could write better poetry than that," but remain wannabe writers because they don't know how to write queries or proposals and where to send them, what editors look for in manuscripts, or how to manage their time to make wishes reality. And those who do complete a novel or article need help with the follow-through on how to get published. Editors don't have time to tutor.

Some of the how-to topics cover: trade books, essays, broadcast documentaries, blogs, textbooks, poetry, columns, screenplays, YA novels, profiles, book reviews, newsletters, articles, memoirs, children's books, and educational support materials.

Articles such as transferring classroom skills, workshops, networking, research, freelancing, agents, self-publishing, and author websites will guide the educator to successful fiction or nonfiction publication. The insider's look includes using style formats, how to work with newspapers and magazines, educational market guidelines, how to fit writing into professional and personal life, writing for professional acceptance, editing your own work, keeping a diary, what to watch in poetry contests, contemporary multicultural and social issues, collaboration—as well as needed encouragement.

Educators as *Writers: Publishing for Personal and Professional Development* is organized into: (I) Getting Started, (II) Submitting Your Work, (III) Working with Publishers, (IV) Non-book Writing, (V) Book Writing, and (VI) Writing Life of a Professional. Eighteen coauthors have each written (or cowritten) three articles, making fifty-four articles.

The first article is about becoming a writer, and the last covers the topic of a visiting author. The various elementary-college contributors provide assistance from the beginning of a writing career to successful publication. Their combined years of experience are sure to help the novice and even the experienced writer find new avenues to express creativity.

There is no book currently like this one—written by successful, published educators for other educators.

Carol Smallwood, Editor

Table of Contents

ii   *Submitting Your Work*

iii   *Working with Publishers*

iv *Non-book Writing*

v   *Book Writing*

vi   *Writing Life of a Professional*

i

getting
started

SHARON CHMIELARZ

Becoming a Writer

Sometimes the adage, "When life hands you a lemon, make lemonade," actually fits your life. After twenty years of teaching, I discovered that all non-essential courses in my district were being cut. My position as a German teacher was one of the first to go on the chopping block.

I reacted like any teacher would who wants to hold her job—I went back to school to get another degree. So began my accidental meeting with writing. I decided, since I'd always liked to read, I could teach English. The courses I took were immaterial to me. I liked 4:30 P.M. classes best. I could just make it to the U. after school, take in a lecture, be home by seven to get a meal together, throw in a load and get ready for the next day. One of those classes happened to be a course on Auden and Dylan, chosen not for its content but for its time.

The muse blew my tight, little plans away. Auden awed me. I wanted to write like that. And poetry looked so easy! For a poem you didn't even need to fill a whole page. (The ignorant rush in where angels fear to tread.) What's more, there couldn't be any competition in it; after all, whom did I know who even read poetry?

Some of that naivety cracked during my first poetry-writing workshop. Hmmm. This was going to entail more than I'd thought. Also, everyone in the workshop (all much younger than I) knew every poet the poet-teacher referred to. Everyone had already had experience, however minor, in getting published. Unconsciously at first, I began setting up a strategy to catch up, small goals, and baby steps.

For example, my classmates raved about a local independent bookstore in St. Paul. I'd never heard of it. I was determined to find it. I did and browsed its books and literary magazines. Reading writing magazines exposed me to opportunities I wouldn't have otherwise known about. Some magazines were locally published; I set a goal to send work to them. I also found ads for "summer camps" for writers, or workshops. I set a goal to apply for Breadloaf. One goal led to another. To get to know other writers, I attended as many readings in bookstores and our local literary center, the Loft, as I could. I wanted to make writer friends; I discovered via word of mouth and newspapers that many local writers also taught workshops. I enrolled. I got to know them and they, me. Fellow workshop participants widened my circle of acquaintances; some have become my very best friends.

I wanted, too, to find out what was hot on the market. I read. I *bought* books and read them. I parted at first with my hard earned cash like a miser parting with a gold piece. Was this really necessary? (Yes.) And because I wanted to have a book published some day, too, I began to collect poems in a folder. Most important to achieve my goals, I wrote. I kept journals, dream journals and notebooks. After supper, which was topped off by three stiff cups of coffee (coffee never kept me from falling asleep), I'd push aside the dishes and reach for a writing notebook. I joined a writers' critique group to improve my skills and through it made more writer friends. (Writer friends are very important. They understand a writer's problems more than your non-writer next-door neighbor or brother or sister.) In short, my goals were realistic and progressive. They didn't include being published in *The New Yorker* (that's still one of my wild goals). Exclusively, outrageously ambitious goals with dates no less would only have led to frustration and defeat.

When I realized what I was doing unconsciously, I made a list of goals.

Some writers put their lists in a dream box. (It's fun to run across these goals after a few years and discover that, yes, you've actually met some of them.) Although I still add goals to the list, I haven't by any means accomplished all of them yet. I think of Robert Browning's, "A man's reach should exceed his grasp, or what's a heaven for?"

Somewhere along the way a writer who wants to be published has to deal with rejects. Some writing teachers suggest collecting enough rejection letters to wallpaper your room. Who would want to be so masochistic? What has helped me in keeping down rejection blues is to conduct the process in a businesslike way. I keep a list of where I've sent what and, most important, I note alternate places to send the work to, should it be rejected. The process then becomes less a commentary on my worth. Work can be returned for any number of reasons. A slow return can often be helpful. Distance in time can give a detached perspective, which helps in revising a submission if it needs more work. It's another way to make lemonade out of a lemon.

When I was new to writing, I wanted someone to tell me that I had loads of talent. No one did. I often heard the comment, "I have to write." I'm not so sure I was born to do anything. I haven't the genius to rise to the very top of the writing pantheon (though I aim for a Pulitzer, my reach will never extend that far). But the very fact that I'm attracted to writing means I have a certain proclivity for it that others don't. More important than talent I've discovered is persistence.

The movie *Amadeus* was released during my early years of writing. In the theater's dark cave, where we're open to all emotions, mine quivered with Salieri's. I understood completely his blasphemous cursing at God for not giving him enough talent to compete with Mozart. Even on my much more humble level, competing with another writer would be dangerous. It would be opting for frustration and an unhealthy competition; in short, misery. My competition has to be with myself. That doesn't preclude having ambitions; but it tempers my ambition to my present and potential capabilities. A good way to go for any writer.

SANDRA SUNQUIST STANTON

2

From Principle to Practical

Workshops inspire me to try new things, matching what I've learned to my professional goals. For lasting benefit, I need to translate the principles into a practical form I can use right away. After training in responsive classroom (RC), my action plan included adapting a program we had developed in our school to apply RC principles. The in-service staff encouraged me to share the program with other RC-trained educators in their "Origins" newsletter.

The publication process began by revisiting Play Fair's goals and objectives, and focusing on principles that reflected RC philosophy. Translating Play Fair's procedures into RC language, I described an end-of-the-year activity I did with several grade levels, and photographed the children during the activity.

The actual writing started with my word map, which became a cursory outline attached to their prescribed word limit. It always helps me to visualize my audience as I write as if talking directly to her. This time, she was a very busy educator trying to grab a brief change of scene between classes, either sitting at a desk or with a cup of coffee in the teachers' lounge. The plan includes the objective, a reference to the applicable state standard, a list of resources, supplies, handouts, necessary equipment, step-by-step process, evaluation procedures, and the time necessary to complete the lesson. Keeping the language simple and direct, I tried to keep thoughts flowing in a logical sequence, offering specific examples, so she could imagine similar activities in her school situation.

Computer tools helped me run the article past my peers who helped me keep everything clear and practical. I typically use the following tools as I write for publication: e-mail attachments, word count, spell check, thesaurus, track changes, inserting date and time, headers and footers, find and replace, PDF files, and digital photography.

Attachments

My computer uses Windows XP, Microsoft 2003, Internet Explorer, and Charter for my Internet server. In order to keep the article's format consistent as we send it back and forth, save and send it as an attachment. With my system, I compose the message, click the attachment paper clip, and have the option to "Browse," (find the saved file) in My Documents, "Open" it, "Attach" it, and "Save" a copy in my "Sent files" as I send it off. Keeping a copy in my files helps me retrace the questions I asked about the piece, which draft I sent, and when I sent it. The best part of this process is meeting at a coffee shop to share the final draft before submitting it for publication.

On each draft of the piece, I note my start and stop time and date, and the number of words. That helps if another publication later wants a shorter or longer version. It also shows my progression and illustrates my process example for other developing writers that I mentor.

The thesaurus and spell check help me catch stray keystrokes and offer other ways to say things that recur throughout a piece.

Headers and Footers/Page Numbers

I want anyone who reads my work to catch the sequence without fumbling through pages. Inserting page numbers, my name, date, and title or topic in the header takes care of that I fasten the pages with a paper clip instead of a staple making it easier to flip through, keeping the pages flat. Any page that needs work can easily be clipped on top of the pile if I need to leave the work for a while.

Track Changes

Using Track Changes makes it easy to distinguish between my original text and my friend's suggestions. I send the attachment; she opens it, saves it, and then goes to "Track Changes" on the upper toolbar. She types her suggestions, saves it again, and attaches it to a return message. After re-opening and reading my copy with her suggestions, I have the option to accept individual changes, or accept or reject all of them at once.

Find and Replace

Editing my work, I sometimes discover that I've misspelled someone's name, or have an acronym wrong. Proofreading an early draft, I realized I had missed some references. Using Windows' "Find and Replace" tool, I clicked on the binoculars to open the tool, entered "PLAY FAIR" (the incorrect format) under "Find." The tool then highlighted each erroneous entry. Next, I clicked on "Replace," entered "Play Fair," and clicked replace again. Voila, they are (theoretically) all fixed.

PDF Files

After my work is published, I ask my editor for a PDF file to save for future use on my own website, or to share with someone else. This step requires software I don't have in my system; but it's available for purchase.

Photography

Reaching a preoccupied reader requires something eye-catching. Digital photography supplies just the right visual accent to my work. Composing artistically pleasing photographs means more than "point and shoot." The most common mistake is not filling the frame. Our eye convinces us that we see what we want to see. When the photo is printed, extra things sometimes show up that didn't catch our attention while shooting. Some professional photographers suggest framing the picture, then taking two steps forward to capture more subject and less surrounding space.

The rule of thirds helps compose a visually interesting shot. Imagine the frame divided into thirds horizontally and vertically. Particularly in landscape photography, place the feature element of the photo at an intersection of these dividing lines. Check out award winning photos—that's their formula.

Some stalwart authors proudly still use typewriters. I can't imagine writing without the convenience of the tools available through technology. Mistakes still happen, but they are much easier to fix this way. Learning continues.

Sharing successful programs from our school with other educators gives us a chance to take another more objective look at a program and tweak it, keeping it fresh. Questions, suggestions, and appreciation make publishing the plan worth the time and effort.

CYNTHIA BRACKETT-VINCENT

3

Getting Published

Starting from Nowhere

I'll be blunt: it seemed that once I *got* published, it was easier to get published again—exactly like a college kid, after receiving that impossible first line of financial credit. Instead of examining why that is—are most editors apt to take a gamble on someone already gambled upon? Is it the practice at the submission/acceptance process that makes a writer better? Perhaps my last name sounds more publishable hyphenated—all these philosophizings are not going to get *you* anywhere. But *knowing* that having those first publication credits under your belt will increase your chances of being published again *is* what matters.

What you should not do is 1. Dash off a submission right now (first, learn from others' mistakes in my third chapter! [Chapter 14]) nor 2. Dash it off to just anyone, especially anyone who wants your money (read my subsequent chapter so you don't get taken). Now that's settled, let's concentrate on how to start.

Here's a good rule to start with: quality counts. What I mean is: for example, a respectable college newsletter, newspaper, or journal is, to my mind, more highly regarded as credits go, than, let's say, your neighborhood news bulletin. A contributor to a college newspaper usually receives no monetary compensation (but rather as many copies as she can hoard or hand out). The neighbors might pay you $20 to write your bulletin. So, compensation will not necessarily become your guiding force. You will get a feel for the hierarchy of publishing credits.

Another rule: write what you know. How many times have we heard this? To put this into action, write an article/a poem about/for a group you are very familiar with. Write with their newsletter/journal/magazine in mind. Examples: your church or denomination, college alumni association, professional organization, outdoor recreation club, conservation organization, hobby (think sports/food/wine/crafts/pets/travel) organization, charity, and so on. If you are invested in any way, you are the perfect person to write that piece!

Now that your mind is racing with ideas, write them down, then slow down—think through how your piece will be interesting and fresh. What insight do you have that is unique? Importantly, what subject has *not* been written about lately that is just waiting for you to tackle it? Resist the urge to submit just yet. Writing that article, essay, or poem on your favorite subject is just that—the focused writing begun. Following are many ideas to help you seek out your first publishing opportunities—perfect for those in academic and professional fields.

Volunteer to Edit

Volunteer to edit a newsletter, newspaper, or journal. This can include any of the above examples. Most of these endeavors will not refuse helping hands! "Editing" can be: helping to proofread, making suggestions regarding copy or content, and logging in submissions and weeding through submissions. Volunteering to edit is an invaluable experience because you will get to see the publishing process from the other side of its desk. When you are ready to submit to such places, you'll know exactly what editors look for, and chances are, you'll be attuned to editors' pet peeves as well! Best of all: you now have real experience as an editor to put on your list of credits when you send out work. When I was a community college student, I helped to edit its newspaper. My name appeared side by side with the former college president. I've also edited my church and church's district newsletters. Responsibilities in each one varied (from laying out articles to interviewing, to actual copyediting) and each experience not only taught me lessons, but also gave me credibility when I started a poetry journal. Poems or articles from editors are commonplace and you can usually include one as such— but check first to see if you'd be overstepping your boundaries. Your volunteer experience may pay off doubly—you might rack up publishing *and* editing experience in one place.

Network

We network in our business life. To become serious about publishing, network. Your first goal is to become familiar with what's going on around you. For example, if you write poetry, where do other poets start? Where are they reading their work and where are they publishing for the first time? How on earth did they make that connection? Many assume "open mics" are for poetry only, or for experienced readers only. Nothing could be further from the truth. Lots of open mics encourage readers of fiction and writers of songs as well as poetry and *most of them* are supportive of beginners. Attend once before you commit to reading—is it the type of environment you'd be comfortable in? If you can't muster up the courage to read, talk to people whom you've admired at an open mic. Ask for advice; many of us are happy to share stories of our first publications (especially if admiration is involved). Open mics and literary readings are often places that startup journals put out "calls for submissions"—poetry, fiction, or nonfiction. You may be able to speak with the editor of a startup about her new venture. Take home a copy of any information she has available. You can also volunteer to help edit a new journal. It would be equivalent to an "unpaid internship" but you would be able to see journals such as your future markets in a new light. Make sure the editor knows you're not looking for your name on the credit page or to become a business partner—that you're a professional in your own field, looking for experience in the literary world.

Join (or start) a writers' group. This is another fantastic way to network with like-minded people. Look in your local newspaper for such groups; do some investigating or visiting—if you can't find a group to suit your needs, start one. You want people who write similar genres (not similar styles, as the more you are exposed to, the better your writing will become). You want other members who will commit to supporting each other, perhaps by traveling to literary readings together; perhaps by workshopping; and perhaps by helping each other to become published writers. Find out how other successful writing groups accomplish their goals and come up with a mission statement and organizational structure to suit your needs. (And don't forget personal rules of safety when meeting with new people.)

Attend a creative writing class to better your craft and to make contacts. You can do this at many levels (and levels of monetary output): *the adult education level*—frequently taught by retired professors or local authors at a very low cost to community participants; *the community college level*—inexpensive as colleges go but academically challenging; *the college and university levels*—prices more expensive (but range widely), academic expectations higher, professors more well-known, accomplished writers. Many of these classes can be taken even if one is not enrolled in a degree program at the college, but some classes have prerequisites. Frequently the professors of these classes will arrange panels to talk to students about publishing opportunities; frequently one of the exercises assigned will be (guided) practice in sending out submissions. Some of your fellow students may have already been published. Learn all you can from these golden opportunities!

Once that poem or article is ready, where (exactly) to start? Start small! Start with new journals you learn of through networking. Beginning journals need submissions. Start where you know others got their start—others whose work is comparable to your own. Start local. Peruse the directories, such as *Poet's Market* (F&W Publications); *The Directory of Poetry Publishers; International Directory of Little Magazines and Small Presses* (Dustbooks) and, the invaluable resource, *Small Press Review* (*SPR*) (also from Dustbooks). In the first three (annuals), one can find magazines, journals, and publishers by their geographic locations. It's a good idea to start with those in one's own area. You know the region. After you think you've found a potential market, make certain it is appropriate for your work (more in my third chapter). The last, *SPR*, a bimonthly newsletter, lists new magazines in each issue, and the editors not only review new small press releases, but also they recommend markets. *SPR* contains *The Small Magazine Review*— a wonderful starting point—also with recommendations. Don't overlook

"The Markets" section of *Writer's Digest,* nor advice in *WD,* and in *Poets and Writers Magazine.*

Start with markets that are open to beginners. You don't necessarily have to start with new journals, or local/regional journals. Many journals are open to beginners. In *Poet's Market,* for example, listings are coded as to openness to beginners. The editors who have listings in this publication frequently give tips for new writers. Start where you think your chances are good. Don't overlook the Internet for searching out markets.

There's a whole world of us who took that first impossible step. Follow these suggestions and new writers will be asking you, "Where/how did you first get published?" Imagine your thrill as *you* give the advice!

SUZANNE L. BUNKERS

4

Keeping a Diary

Keeping a diary is a personal activity that can also help you immensely in your work as a writer. Your diary can be formal and stylized or conversational and idiomatic. In your diary, you can not only record your ideas for stories but also reflect on your need for self-affirmation, your quest for knowledge, and the wish to make your mark on the world as a writer.

This essay will offer specific suggestions for "jump-starting" your writing, reflecting on personal experiences and their relationship to your writing, and coping with writer's block. In addition, online diary sites will be recommended. Let's begin by exploring basic information on the diary.

What is a diary? When I began doing research on diaries twenty years ago, I made a distinction between the diary as a form for the recording of events and the journal as a form for introspection, reflection, and the expression of feelings. Like many others, I have found this to be an artificial distinction, both as the result of my research and as the result of my own diary keeping over the past forty years.

In fact, there are as many kinds of diaries as there are diarists. A diary might be kept in a tiny hard-covered book with lock and key, but it might just as easily be kept in a spiral notebook, on loose-leaf paper, or on the backsides of used envelopes. A diary entry might consist of a one-line report on daily events, but it might just as often consist of a three-page analysis of one's beliefs, attitudes, and desires. Many diaries, especially those kept over a number of years, contain both kinds of entries.

Who writes in a diary? Diaries can have many different kinds of authors. Some diaries have individual authors and appear to have been written for the diarist only. Some diaries have individual authors but also indicate that, besides the diarists themselves, selected family members or friends might be allowed to read (or even write) entries in the diaries. Other diaries exemplify multiple authorship maintained over decades and generations. Such diaries can function as family or communal diaries—texts written as a family or community record and often preserved in private homes as well as in historical society archives.

Why is the diary so alluring, especially to us as writers? The diary's allure is linked to its elasticity. Diary entries can be formal and stylized and/or conversational and idiomatic. The diary can reflect its author's need for self-affirmation, quest for knowledge, desire to make one's mark on the world, and/or journey through change and loss. A diary can function as a therapeutic tool as well as a record of daily events, thereby providing insights into the diarist's self-image as well as his or her interactions with others. Why? Because the form and content of a diary are shaped not only by its writer's personality but also by her or his experience of race, ethnicity, class, age, sexual orientation, and geographic setting.

As you read diaries written by other individuals, and as you begin keeping your own diary, you may wish to consider these questions:

- Why am I drawn to read of another person's daily experiences?
- What makes the idea of keeping a diary appealing to me as a writer?
- What can diaries help me appreciate about the experiences of the individuals who kept them?
- What can my own tell me, not only about the reasons why I write in my diary, about my privacy requirements for keeping a diary, about whether I am willing to share my diary with others?

- What is my relationship to my diary if it is edited and published?

In her recent book, *Leaving a Trace: On Keeping a Journal* (2001), Alexandra Johnson outlines ten patterns found in diaries:

Journals contain ten categories of life patterns: longing; fear; mastery; (intentional) silences; key influences; hidden lessons; secret gifts; challenges; unfinished business; untapped potential. Each category corresponds to a way we engage or hold back in life. To begin to see a journal through these ten organizing devices is to unknot years of tangled entries. It's most helpful if you go back through journals first by posing each life pattern as a question. (p. 125)

When I advise other writers about how to begin keeping a diary, I recommend several books on the subject, including Tristine Rainer's *The New Diary*, Christina Baldwin's *Life's Companion*, and Alexandra Johnson's *Leaving a Trace*. In addition, I like to make suggestions for subjects to be explored in specific diary entries. Here are six of my favorite suggestions:

1   Write about one belief or value that you hold in high esteem. Define what this belief or value is. Next, write about why it is important to you now. Finally, write about how and why it has become important to you.

2   Think about the first "safe place" you remember. It might have been the kitchen or parlor in your childhood home; it might have been your own room; it might have been another place. Write about this place, describing how it looked, sounded, and smelled. Then, write about how you feel as you remember it now.

3   If you could travel anywhere and be in one place that is very special to you, where would it be? Describe how this place looks, sounds, and smells as you remember it. Then describe the feelings you have as you remember it.

4   Write about a time when you felt like an outsider who didn't belong. Remember where you were and with whom; then write about those details. Afterwards, write about the feelings that come back to you now as you remember the experience.

5   Write about a time when you had to "take a stand" that was unpopular with your partner, a family member, a friend, and a colleague. First, recall the experience, writing down a list of sights, sounds, smells, etc. Then write about the details of the situation and your

need to "take a stand." Finally, write about your feelings as you reflect on the experience now.

6   Write about a "Road Taken" or a "Road Not Taken." First, write about what you remember. Then, write about how it feels to you now as you reflect on the experience.

In the introduction to *Diaries of Girls and Women: A Midwestern American Sampler,* I write about the new world of the online diary:

> The recent explosion of communication via electronic media has resulted in hundreds of diaries being kept on the World Wide Web. When one analyzes what it means to keep one's diary on the Web, thereby making each entry accessible to a potentially huge international readership, reconceptualizing the diary and the act of diary keeping itself becomes even more important. Questions of purpose and audience inevitably become far more complex. Why? Because time-worn assumptions that the diary is being kept only for the diarist and that it is an intensely secretive and private enterprise are unworkable when exploring the phenomenon of the online diary. (p. 27)

You might wish to explore this burgeoning world of the online diary by reading diaries kept by individuals on such online clearinghouse websites as The Diary Registry, The Diary Project, and The Online Diary History Project. If you have access to a computer, you can keep your own online diary. Here are several of my favorite online sites:

The Open Diary
http://www.opendiary.com

The Diary Project
http://www.diaryproject.com

The Diary Registry
http://www.diarist.net/registry

Diaryland.com
www.diaryland.com

The Online Diary History Project
ttp://216.92.219.220/introduction.htm

Sources Cited

Baldwin, Christina (1990). *Life's Companion: Journal Writing as a Spiritual Quest.* New York: Bantam Books.

Bunkers, Suzanne L. (2001). Introduction. *Diaries of Girls and Women: A Midwestern American Sampler* (Ed. Suzanne L. Bunkers). Madison: University of Wisconsin Press, pp. 3–40.

Johnson, Alexandra (2001). *Leaving a Trace: On Keeping a Journal.* New York: Little, Brown.

Rainer, Tristine (1978). *The New Diary: How to Use a Journal for Self-Guidance and Expanded Creativity.* Los Angeles: J. P. Tarcher, Inc.

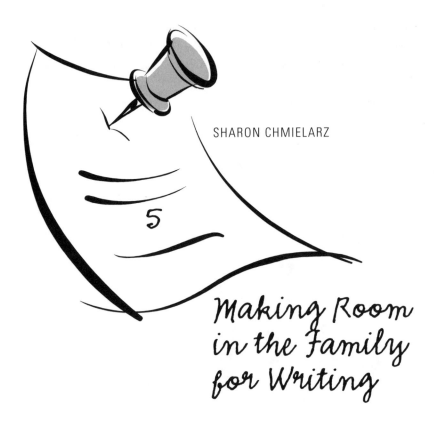

SHARON CHMIELARZ

5

Making Room in the Family for Writing

We were having an argument, one of those storms that continued to roil silently after the lights were out. We lay in bed, each of us well to our side. Then I pulled my blanket and pillow, and streamed to the living room couch. Eventually HE followed. "C'mon," he coaxed, "come back to bed."

Today I haven't the vaguest idea what the fight was about. I do remember we were in the same room but on different planets. "What is it you want?" His voice wrung itself out asking me. What was it I wanted? I opened my mouth. A barely audible croak fell out. " . . . to write."

That startled me as much as him. Did I say that?

"Is that all?" He laughed, relieved. "Write, then! Who's stopping you?"

Little did either I or my husband know that my writing would require major shifts in family time and habits. Families, typically, don't respond to change readily.

Initially my venture seemed unobtrusive. I needed a desk. I mean, a desk of my own. Not the one that stored bills and last year's leftover holiday cards. At the very least, I needed a computer file kept for my writing alone. No one else uses it. No one. My first writing desk was a three-foot-high chest with a board laid across it. I placed an old electric typewriter exactly in the middle of this teeter-totter to balance it. Shaky as it was, it established my territory. (Writers are very lucky when it comes to acquiring equipment when compared, for example, to the visual artist. If we really had to, we could get by with pen and paper.)

The second thing I needed (and you need, too) was a place of my own for this desk. Even if it's the broom closet, it had to be a place with a door.

Consider the following house scenario: You're sitting before your keyboard or yellow tablet. Except for your hands, from Viewpoint #2, you do not look busy in the normal sense. You're just sitting. You may even just be staring at the wall. You look, from that second viewpoint, interruptible. What would be the harm in asking you one, little question? You are there. The question is a pressing one to Viewpoint #2.

Voilà the door. Closed. To keep you out of sight and circumvent interruptions.

Even households where both partners write professionally, and therefore understand the writing process, have to establish formal, uninterrupted territory. It's a working condition that prevents resentments galore. Pete Hautman and Mary Logue do not write in the same room. And during their writing hours they don't allow questions during breaks like, "What's in the dryer?" "When are we eating?" "What's your schedule today?" You may even want to post your writing hours on the door. The sign is a variation on repetition. We writers have to establish ourselves, as we have had to establish classroom rules. The family may find our hours easy to understand but hard to comply with. Life inside the house is far more compatible though when establishing your space: closing the door without bombast, threats, martyrdom or, that killer of domestic tranquility, door slams.

A simple, quiet persistence, in words and action, works . . . unless it doesn't. Then you may have to rent a writing space (maybe you live in a town with a literary center like the Loft in Minneapolis) or use a cubicle in the library or plan on making multiple writing retreats (read your writing magazines for their ads) or write in coffeehouses. We're serious about writing whether we look at the commitment as an apprenticeship, a part-time or full-time position. If we persist, the family will eventually modify their behavior.

I discovered the biggest block in my family to my writing was right inside my head. An inner, critical voice. The critic was as interruptive as exterior voices. For example, that small voice reacts immediately when a money button is pushed. As a teacher, I'm used to receiving a salary for my work. As a writer, publication may lend me a certain authority, but not money.

This is a big, mental adjustment. I remember the first acceptance letter I received. I'd sent in a poem about one of my students to a teacher's magazine. I was ecstatic with the response. I called my parents long distance. My dad answered. My dad, the union man. His first question: "How much did you get?"

That inner voice tells us that since we're earning no money, our writing time can't be so very important. When the first rejection slip comes in, the small voice gets louder. Not only are we not earning anything, but also our work isn't good enough to get accepted. At best, our writing is a preoccupation, a hobby, so how have we the audacity, the gall, to close the door and postpone the meal? Who do we think we are, anyway?

My critical voice also exploited my family to whom the literary world was terra incognita. In childhood, the closest I came to that world was in the classroom (textbooks) and public library (books for leisure but who thought of the authors behind them?). My family's library consisted of the Bible on the coffee table and a stack of catalogs on a shelf. The latter were by far the most thumbed. The most intellectual person I knew as a child was Uncle Mike who subscribed to *National Geographic*.

For years, my critical voice used this as a stumbling block. The only successful writers, my critic reasoned, were born into literary or intellectual families. Their mothers read to them at bedtime, their fathers owned studies, their aunts' and uncles' pedigrees included a list of titles and books they'd written, and they themselves had attended five star colleges. Had I come from a family like this, there'd be no question of having my own desk and door in a family like this, but I did not.

The more I wrote and read though, the more instances of similar background I found. Two very famous and wonderful poets come to mind instantly: James Wright and Theodore Roethke. Every genre has its share.

Controlling that critical, inner-family voice is essential. Its (trained) skills are useful only during revision. What counts is the actual writing and getting your work to the eyes of someone who can help it come to print. And for that you need a desk and space and time in a relatively compatible setting.

Of course, there are times when writers must compromise with family to keep harmony. We moved recently and for months before and the week after we moved, I wrote by the seat of my pants. My writer friends assured me I'd be able to get back into the groove. Whenever I did have time during those weeks of preparation and then actual moving, I usually felt too unsettled to do fresh writing. So I took care of the business end of writing. If a creative idea came on, I jotted it down on whatever scrap of paper flew by. I lowered my expectations: I felt successful if I got the idea into a computer file at day's end.

Moving, divorce, family illnesses or deaths disorient us at the desk as much as they would in the classroom. As writers, we have an advantage in flexibility over the classroom teacher. We can't assemble our students at midnight for a missed hour though we can sit down at our desk and work.

When Judy Delton began writing, she was a newly divorced mother with four young children. She set her typewriter on the dining room table, set up working hours, and announced, "From now on, I earn our living as a writer, and you four will have to take care of the house." It worked. She became the author of countless books for children and her own children grew in confidence and competence.

I was still using my teeter-totter desk the afternoon I got the call that my first poetry book manuscript had been accepted for publication. The day happened to be our twenty-fourth wedding anniversary. I remember jumping like a kid as I held the wall phone in the kitchen. I remember my husband coming up behind me, his expression asking what had happened. I remember feeling much happier about the book than the anniversary celebration. And I remember his face falling when he realized my delight had nothing to do with him. Never mind that I'd dedicate that book to him. The moment was hugely telling.

Writing is a new passion or an old one revived. In the end, acknowledging it forthrightly to our family as something we want to do creates more harmony in the long run than letting the passion silently grow into an elephantine presence knocking down the walls to be seen in our house.

MAGGIE MIESKE

6

prepare to Be published

William Maxwell once said, "A writer is a reader who is moved to emulation." As soon as I learned to read, I wanted to write. It didn't matter if it was short stories or poetry. If I could read it, I could write it: in the third grade, I won a short-story writing contest.

Reading (and Writing) Is Still Fundamental

Reading is an essential part of writing and thus essential to preparation for publication. I have read everything I could set my eyes on and found opportunities to write from grade school. I have researched and written articles and term papers. I have kept journals of vacations, bird watching, dieting and difficult periods of my life. I have compiled lists for shopping and setting and doing goals and especially enjoy "honey-do" lists for my husband.

I have written poems that sometimes became stories and stories that sometimes became poems, and some that were accomplished on the spot of the napkin. I have expressed my satisfaction or my disappointment in letters to the editors of newspapers or newsletters, employers or managers of hotels including letters to my loved ones and a few not-so-loved ones.

It All Adds Up

I have watched people and animals and sunsets; breathed fresh air and stale air; smelled flowers and pines and sunshine; listened to birds, ripples on a pond and waves crashing on the shore of Lake Michigan; felt the velvet nose of my horse and the hot sand of the beach between my toes; and have shared butterfly kisses with my granddaughter.

All of these everyday things are fodder for the writer's pen (or keyboard)—if you write it and write it well, they will read it.

However you manage to arrive at the conclusion that it's time to start submitting your work, the key is to keep writing and to keep submitting. Keep in mind that it may take a thousand rejections before you receive one acceptance.

Advantages of Publication

Let's face it. Being published "looks good." It looks good to prospective editors, universities, professors, employers and scholarship committees. It feels good, too. It boosts confidence and self-esteem and makes a better writer. What are you waiting for?

Where Do You Start?

If you don't own one yourself, your first important investment when you are ready to start submitting is a *Poet's Market* or *Writer's Market,* which you should be able to find or have ordered for you at any bookstore. They should also be available online through places such as Amazon.com. One costs around thirty dollars but is absolutely invaluable if you are serious about submitting your work for publication. They are updated and published annually so you will want a recent copy. The *Poet's Market* is only about 500 plus pages but there are hundreds of entries (nearly 2000 publishers) and the *Writer's Market* is even larger. In addition, they include articles on writing cover letters and book proposals, plus tips and issues related to writing in different genres. Another excellent source of publishers is *The International Directory of Little Magazines & Small Presses.*

From the Beginning

Get yourself a highlighter and start going through one starting with A or your venue of choice. Highlight the publishers who are willing to publish new poets/writers. Learn the key to the symbols in the front of the book and you won't have any trouble. Take a moment when skimming through to see what publishers' needs are. If they want political satire or comment in their poetry and you write nature stuff, that is probably not one you want to highlight. This author tries to find the editors who also state they offer comments.

Choosing Your First

When exhaustion sets in and your fingertips glow from your favorite highlighter color, stop! Go back through your highlighted entries, read them over again very carefully and pick two or three or even four that sound like quality publications. Go to the trouble of sending for sample copies of those that interest you. It might save you the embarrassment later of finding yourself published in a sloppy rag with poor proofreading, horrible poetry or even something X-rated that you would never have considered had you seen a sample first.

Don't Forget

Read the publisher's "How to Submit" paragraph (take note of their views on cover letters, simultaneous submissions and previously published poems) and their notes of "Advice" before you submit so you don't make any major boo-boos. Even minor boo-boos can cost you a reading and your work will be axed before it ever hits the editor's desk. Don't waste your time or risk ticking off an editor with carelessness.

Submission Logs

Keep track of what you have submitted and where on a log or in the margins of the book of publishers that you use. You don't want to waste your time submitting the same thing twice because it would not go over well with the editor. Eventually, you will receive an acceptance that should substitute for caffeine and/or Prozac for several days thereafter. When that wears off and you've had a few more rejections, submit again.

"Be persistent. Editors change; editorial tastes change; markets change. Too many beginning writers give up too easily." (John Jakes)

Take Your Time

Read the comments editors take time to give. You might not like some while others may give you just the right idea for revision. Don't take comments personally and don't make revisions for an editor because you are desperate to be published. If you are committed to the integrity of a poem or story and truly feel it must remain as is, then submit it elsewhere. Once it is published, it is published and later revisions will appear unprofessional and either indicate you didn't put time into revision in the first place or that you aren't as committed to your work as you should be. It is okay to disagree with an editor.

It's also worthwhile to keep *all* of your work, submitted, rejected, finished or unfinished to come back to at a later date. It may be just the thing you are looking for and time and perspective may give you the inspiration to finish or revise it perfectly.

Mentors Matter

Hopefully, someone you know may have already gone through some of this process and can give you encouragement, support and advice. A mentor is a gem you won't want to miss if the opportunity presents itself. A mentor may be a published author or poet you admire and that you might be lucky enough to meet in a class, a workshop or at a reading. Another way to find a mentor might be through an online database for your state such as Michigan Authors and Illustrators. Your next-door neighbor, your mail carrier or your chiropractor might be a poet or a humor essayist.

SHARON CHMIELARZ

7

Transferring Classroom Skills onto the Page

Many of the skills I learned as a classroom teacher morphed into those needed by a writer. Among others, showing not telling, writing plot and story like a lesson plan progression, using personal experience as style and content, practicing patience, treating each student or article as a unique personality, keeping the audience in mind, and remembering the necessity for clarity and personal discipline.

Let's look at each more closely. One of the first catch phrases in a writing workshop is the old chestnut, "Show don't tell." A teacher knows already how this works in the classroom. Who has ever taught a student basketball by handing him/her a book? "Read it by Friday, our first game." The student uses hands-on technique to get the feel of the ball and running down a court. Just so, the reader has to get the feel of a story. The bare facts she/he already intuits, for example friendless new student finally meets friend. In writing, "hands-on" is equivalent, connecting with readers through feeling:

conveying emotion. Telling them, for example, "I lost," is not going to hit them in the pit of their stomachs nearly as well as showing how that feels.

Some writers don't use a plotline. They begin a story with a character so compelling they must write about her/him. They have no idea where the story will go or what's going to happen in it. They follow their character to find out. Other writers know the ending before they sit down to write the beginning. Whatever technique you employ, at some point an outline is helpful, and it's not unlike a lesson plan. As a teacher, I wrote one at the end of each week, turning in a copy (required) and revising as the new week progressed, adjusting the pace for my students' learning. When I write a long piece now an outline is helpful to me; with it I can remember what has happened to the character and watch the story's arc. Does the character encounter problems? Does the tension hit a peak? Is there an exciting or satisfactory resolution? Teachers do this quite naturally in the classroom; a teacher-writer transfers it to the art of writing.

How many times have teachers caught a student's drifting attention by dropping an anecdote? It's an old trick, use of personal experience. If overused, it's a time waster; if used in moderation, it's effective in creating classroom bonds as well as motivation. Having varied experiences makes the teacher seem human, even vulnerable. Having varied experiences deepens the writer's work. We can understand our subject's or character's emotions by recalling our personal experience. Love, fear, resentments, and loss are emotions everyone share. You're not sure how the character who steals feels? What were your emotions when you were dared to shoplift as a teenager? Although the writer is not the character, writers draw on their own emotions and experience to flesh out their subjects.

Of course, experience can be effectively created from imagination. One of Robert Bly's earlier poems uses the metaphor of a woman in a cave; in it Bly calls her his wife. Once, after a reading, an audience member came up and was concerned that Mrs. Bly sat in a cave. In this case, the poet's metaphor didn't match his life experience but its effect was vivid nonetheless.

Patience! How we need it in the classroom. How we need it at the writing desk. Our stories, articles, essays, poems, and novels do not hatch at the rate we want them to. The editor doesn't respond quickly enough. Our skills don't mature as fast as we'd like. The ink cartridge runs out just when we need to run off copies. Our writing time runs out, and we have to leave our desks to get to another job, appointment, etc. The family is insisting on a meal

now, and we want to finish a chapter. The editing of a particular piece is taking longer than we thought it would. In all these cases, patience is required:
we define what we can do at that moment and attend to it. We learn this in
the classroom. Each individual or story needs its own time to come to
fruition. Writers learn to have as much patience with themselves as teachers with students.

When I write, I rarely think of a reader. I'm following an idea which
appeals to me, the childish me, who writes about what she likes. *After* I have
a draft, however, remembering the audience is extremely helpful in editing.
I think of you, a colleague, a fellow teacher, as I write this article, and it helps
shape what I say. When I write for children, I remember their ages and faces.
The classroom teacher understands this. Teaching a second grader requires
a different approach from teaching a ninth grader or college sophomore. The
writer imagines a conversation with the reader. Without talking down or up,
she/he delivers a story or information in a manner and style which catches
and holds that age group's interest. The teacher strives to do this everyday
in class.

If a teacher has the courage to walk into a classroom of students and keep
the instruction rolling for an entire nine months over an obstacle course of
student absences, testing, administrative decrees, changes in the daily
schedule, field trips, intercom interruptions, etc., the teacher-writer will find
the course on the page a breezeway. Your biggest obstacle may be the lack
of peer evaluation. (Writing groups fill this blank.) You've faced a-loneness
in the classroom, where evaluations of your skills were few and far between.
You know how the classroom teems with emotions and goals and interruptions. Every day as a writer, now, you face the page, a possibility of teeming
emotions, goals, hopes, and failures. Yet you discipline yourself to walk in
daily, sit down, and pick up the pen.

The object is clarity. In the classroom, no matter what teaching techniques you used, the object was clarity. Can the student understand, that is
learn what is being required of him/her? The same standard reigns on the
page. Does the reader understand? If not, revision, re-seeing it yourself, and
re-presenting it are required.

I'll remember forever the first night of the first writing class I took at our
local university. I stood outside the classroom door and looked in. I was in
my navy wool blazer, button-down shirt, gray flannel skirt, nylons, and navy
blue pumps. Ms. Prim and Proper. The instructor half sat, half leaned on the

desk. He was a wiry-shaped hippie, wearing a black and red checkered wool shirt-jacket. His hair was drawn back into a ponytail, and he smoked a cigarillo, squinting when he inhaled. My glance drifted over the ensemble of seven students in the first two rows. If I walked in, they would be my fellow students, my competition. Their clothing style was, well, relaxed. They were all at least fifteen years younger than I. Now was the decision moment. I could walk in, take a seat, and learn how to write a poem, or I could turn around, get a refund, and go home. How much did I want to write?

That night the seeds of persistence were planted, and they were rewarded. Although I didn't know it then, I was extremely lucky. One, because the class was so small, I didn't need a portfolio for admission. This was good because I had none. Two, I walked in on one of the Midwest's best poets, Thomas McGrath, who just happened to be substitute teaching that quarter. And Thomas McGrath was a perfect teacher for a beginner like me; he didn't even blink at my very bad poems and encouraged me to "read and write," a goal that was in the realm of my capabilities. (It is a continual goal; basic as "keep your eye on the ball" to a tennis player.)

I'd walked into a class where my relaxed colleagues had been writing for at least as long as they were younger than I. I had come into the class with no skills, I thought. This was one course, I told myself that first night, setting my teeth, I wouldn't ace out. What I discovered was I needed to lean on the skills I'd learned as a classroom teacher while incorporating the skills, which are strictly literary.

Will willingness make anyone a successful writer? No. You still need persistence, luck, a dash of talent, and even more persistence. You need to affix the rear to the chair. You need to face the page the same way you face the classroom daily. You are Daniel entering the lions' den, and the outcome is anything but sure. But your classroom skills are present and ready at your fingertips to be used. Why wouldn't you take command and enjoy using them?

GLORIA D. HEINEMANN

8

Transitioning from Academic to Creative Writing

"How do you use words to get readers to feel an emotion or see something beautiful? Do you have to write when you're 'in the throws' of the emotion or when you're in that beautiful place to capture it for readers?" These are questions I asked myself as I attempted to expand my academic and professional writing and publishing into creative nonfiction.

I've always loved to write and thoroughly enjoyed composition classes in high school and college. My teachers and professors encouraged me, but one professor told me that having an academic degree would give me something worthwhile about which to write, and, as a result, I became a professional nurse and a sociologist with a specialty in social gerontology. During my various careers, writing and publishing were expectations. I've written and published speeches, chapters in edited books, and articles in refereed journals and professional newsletters. I also co-edited and co-wrote a book related to my work with health care teams.

Professionally, I'm a health educator and researcher at the Veterans Affairs (VA) hospital and a faculty member at the University at Buffalo in Buffalo, NY. Two years ago, I began thinking about retirement and what I would do with my time when I no longer have to be in my office every day. I decided I'd like to "try my hand" at full-time freelance writing. When I attempted to write about my personal experiences and feelings, however, my pieces sounded flat. I realized that this kind of writing requires something from me that my academic writing does not. I tried to write about the beauty of the ocean waves pounding the shore, something I'd experienced on a recent vacation, but my words didn't do it justice. I had much to learn.

On a whim, I signed up for a two-day summer writing program at the University of Wisconsin, Madison. I listened intently to the keynote speakers—two well-known writers explaining how they'd become successful. I learned about "hooks" and "leads" in a variety of afternoon workshops and browsed through the books for sale, books written by the keynoters and local faculty, who teach writing at the university and were sponsoring and teaching this summer program. Motivated and energized, I returned home to Buffalo and began writing short pieces about my father. I read them to friends who smiled and praised my efforts, but I needed to know how to improve them. I needed to find a local writers' group, a writers' community.

I began searching through *The Buffalo News* and community newspapers for activities related to writing. Friends and colleagues referred me to their friends and colleagues. I also contacted the University at Buffalo's English Department and Adult Education Program and inquired at major bookstores in and around Buffalo. Several sources suggested I to contact the Just Buffalo Literary Center, which I joined immediately to receive its monthly newsletter.

From these contacts, I learned that my university and several of the smaller colleges and universities in the area occasionally sponsored writing seminars and workshops featuring writers from the New York City area. The Just Buffalo Literary Center also offered a workshop series taught by a local, self-taught writer. From these workshops and an e-mail mentoring program with the local writer, I learned about the different types of nonfiction writing (e.g., personal essays, opinion pieces, travel articles, feature articles, and short stories). I began to develop some of the skills I needed to become a creative writer and to understand the steps involved in getting published. In the workshops, I met others interested in creative writing and became an active member of several local writers' groups.

The following summer, I returned to the University of Wisconsin for its week-long summer writing institute, where I learned about becoming a self-employed freelance writer working from home. Fifteen of us freelance "wannabes" learned to think of writing as a business and to set up a home office. We practiced writing cover and query letters to newspaper, magazine, and book editors and critiqued one another's manuscripts under the guidance of a full-time freelance writer invited to the institute as a guest faculty member.

I learned that being a good, published academic writer isn't enough to guarantee me success as a creative writer. Preparing a theoretical or research article or writing about an area of professional expertise requires different skills than writing from the heart, imagination, or personal experience. I needed to identify skills I already possessed that I could use in creative writing (e.g., reviewing and synthesizing information and interviewing) and continue developing new skills, including how to market myself and my work.

I began to understand the different ways academic and creative writers exhibit creativity. An academic expresses creativity in the development of theory or the design, implementation, and interpretation of research. Write ups generally follow a canned formula or outline, beginning with an abstract and description of the research and ending with implications of findings, summary, and conclusions, determined by professional journal or book editors. In contrast, the creative writer is not only creative in developing characters and plot and describing places and states of mind, but also in the writing process itself. While the academic writer uses a formal writing style and adheres closely to the rules of good writing, the creative writer more often uses a conversational style with shorter sentences, dialogue, and fewer three and four syllable words (i.e., a lower readability level). Creative writers can take more liberties bending and sometimes breaking the rules of good writing to make a point, "conger up" a feeling, and/or create a character or scene.

Writing dialogue between and among characters came relatively easy to me although I'd never attempted it previously. I am an avid reader and a great fan of Robert B. Parker's mysteries set in the Boston area. He uses considerable dialogue among his private investigator, Spencer, a frequent "sidekick" named Hawk, and Spencer's girlfriend, Susan. Reading Parker familiarized me with dialogue and how to use it.

One of my biggest challenges has been to "show" rather than "tell" in my creative writing. As an academic writer, I almost always present information to the reader by describing or telling. To use words to show—to create an emotion or a scene—is new to me. After much critiquing by my writing instructor, I believe I've finally learned to paint pictures with words. I do this most effectively if I carry a journal so I can write when I'm immersed in what I want to write about or when the mood to write strikes me. I look for the details in my observations—for textures and smells as well as visuals. For example, I frequently pen stories about my kitten. I find myself counting the number of breaths she takes in comparison to the number I take in a given time period. I watch her sleep and note the parts of her body that twitch and in what order. I observe her positions, the angle of her head, and how the sun shines on her thick black coat. I feel the warmth of the sun as I run my hand over her soft, silky fur. I find that I use bolder adjectives and more active verbs as a creative writer as well. The effective use of metaphor I'm still attempting to perfect.

Both dialogue and "showing" rather than "telling" are effective writing tools for developing characters. Not only what a character says, but also how he or she says it needs to be communicated to readers. Appearance, clothing, gestures, habits, and idiosyncrasies need to be "spelled out" for readers if they are to see and identify with the writer's characters.

From my own attempts to expand my writing abilities, I offer the following advice. First, find something or someone to motivate you to write, and write on a regular basis, every day if possible. Carry a journal in which to write. Get to know other writers, including some who are more experienced than you are. Listen closely to them and incorporate their feedback in your work. Give other writers feedback; giving feedback reinforces writing skills. Having more than one person critique your work helps you become a well-rounded writer. Read a lot, especially authors who write in your genre. Take workshops and seminars locally, regionally, and nationally. Send your pieces to local publication outlets initially to begin to build your "clips." Don't be afraid of editors; they need you as much as you need them. Last, be persistent. Don't let rejections convince you that can't write. Rewrite your cover or query letter, and submit to another, possibly a more appropriate, publication. Finally, keep it fun, and keep it coming.

Acknowledgment

I dedicate this piece to Kathryn Radeff, freelance writer and writing instructor in Buffalo, NY, and Ft. Myers, FL. She has been a teacher and mentor to me as I've embarked on my new career as a creative writer.

ANN RIEDLING

9

Writing for Professional Acceptance

There will be times throughout your career that you will want to write to organizations, agencies, conferences and so forth for acceptance. Examples include professional (local, national and international conferences), Fulbright programs, special honors and awards, grants and so on. Each of these has specific rules and regulations that must be adhered to. In addition, they typically involve research of some nature. This chapter will explain the strategies, tips and tools that are useful—even necessary—in writing for professional acceptance.

Writing, generally speaking, provides you with an opportunity to conceptualize, explore and reformulate your understanding of a topic. Actually, writing is a simple process if you are willing to relax and allow it to happen. It involves only one non-negotiable component, self-discipline. Determine specific times during the week you can be free to write or conduct research and *honor* those times.

Writing for *professional acceptance* is quite similar to writing for publication. The distinct difference is that you must adhere to specific guidelines provided by the organization or agency to which you are writing. Read and reread these guidelines. Call the organization or agency should you have any questions. Most of them prefer that you ask questions rather than submit a form or proposal that is written incorrectly or is incomplete. They may also provide you with helpful tips.

Writing for professional acceptance is also similar to writing a proposal, a statement relating to a project you would like to accomplish, *persuasive writing*. It is addressed to the agency or organization whose resources will allow you to carry out your project. Your task is to convince them that your project deserves their support. The following are five basic questions that are important to consider when writing for any professional acceptance:

1   What are you going to do?
2   Why does it need to be done?
3   Why do you think you can do it?
4   How are you going to do it?
5   Where have you gone for other information?

For many applications you can discover how the review will be carried out by noticing the questions asked. If they are not asked explicitly, you can anticipate them by imagining yourself as the reviewer.

Writing for professional acceptance varies from short and sweet to extensive and complex. For example, writing for acceptance to present at a local, national or international conference could consist of a single page, requiring your personal information and a brief abstract of what you are going to present. Examples of a submission form to present at a local, national or international conference can be seen at any of the following:

- EDUCAUSE Southeast Regional Conference in Atlanta, Georgia (www.educause.edu/Program/9538).
- American Literature Association in San Francisco, California (www.calstatela.edu/academic/english/ala2/american_literature_2006.html).
- 31st Improving University Teaching (IUT) Annual Forum to Improve Higher Education Conference in Dunedin, New Zealand (www.iutconference.org/callpapers.htm).

In contrast, a Fulbright teaching and/or research scholarship may include personal information, professional working experiences and accomplishments, experiences in living abroad, foreign languages spoken, teaching ability, professional development activities and so forth. In addition, you must complete a Statement of Proposed Research or Teaching, Curriculum Vitae in narrative form and much, much more. This information proceeds through several review processes. You will most likely work closely with your Fulbright advisor during this process (via telephone). Currently, I am a reviewer for Library Science Fulbright proposals (the last stop—reviewing for professionalism in the field of library and information science). In this capacity, I review the submitted proposals for weeks, examining each one in detail to assure that the applicant is suitably knowledgeable in this field of study and can successfully accomplish the proposed mission. Eventually, I select the *one* proposal that meets all criteria most closely. For more information about the Fulbright Scholar Program, visit www.cies.org/us_scholars/guidelines.htm.

Yet another type of writing for acceptance is grant writing. Writing grants is often exceptionally detailed and specific. Numerous courses are offered to assist novice grant writers (online and traditional). These can be extremely helpful. In addition, many articles and websites offer excellent grant writing strategies and procedures. It is vitally important to gain knowledge before writing your first grant. If this is not your first grant, refer to your grant writing resources and closely review the guidelines of the grant to which you are applying.

The "basic overall" components of a grant proposal are:

1   Executive summary
2   Statement of need
3   Project description
4   Budget
5   Organization of information
6   Conclusion

Below are examples of books and websites to get you started with grant writing:

Henson, Kenneth T. (2004). *Grant Writing in Higher Education: A Step-by-Step Guide.* Boston: Allyn & Bacon.

Fox, Arlen Sue and Ellen Karsh (2006). *The Only Grant Writing Book You'll Ever Need: Top Grant Writers and Grant Givers Share Their Secrets!* New York: Carroll & Graf Publishers.

Research Together
www.doctoralstudents.com/location.asp
This site is aimed at all researchers—doctoral students through full-time professors. It includes hundreds of useful forums.

Grant Proposal Writing Tips
www.cpb.org/grants/grantwriting.html
This website is an easy guide to the basic elements of grant proposal writing.

Writing for professional acceptance also includes honors and awards. Often, you must provide personal and professional information and experiences, proposed projects or ventures and so forth. Examples of honors and awards are:

- Award for Instructional Development, Excellence in University Teaching (www.metroversity.org/application.htm).
- American Association of University Women, Promoting Education and Equity for Women Award (www.aauw.org/fga/awards/achieve/cfm).

Writing for professional acceptance is truly a learning experience. It takes practice and patience. Remember, this type of writing is more than *just writing.* It involves following guidelines to a tee, conducting thorough research, talking to others, viewing works that others have submitted, presenting materials *on time,* exercising tenacity and patience, learning from your rejections and never giving up! Many, many people do not receive a grant on the first try. Many people are not accepted to present at an international conference the first time. Most people do not win an honor or award the first time around. That does not equate with failure; it equates with persistence and determination, learning, improving and gaining the knowledge to "win" in the future. Writing for professional acceptance can be one of the most gratifying types of writing in existence. Again, writing is a simple process if you are willing to relax and allow it to happen!

MAGGIE MIESKE

10

Writing Workshops

Prelude to Publishing

Writing is one of those things that usually requires peace, quiet and solitude but writing and revising for potential publication is not always something that can or should be done alone. I didn't start receiving acceptances until creative writing workshops. Since I wanted to continue being accepted and published afterwards, I started my own workshop.

Who Joins a Writing Workshop?

The first ingredient of a successful writing workshop is a group of people committed to writing and sharing their work and to giving and receiving honest criticism. They can come from all walks of life though many are former creative writing students like myself. Some workshops are spawned directly from a creative writing class and include students who get along well and are serious about continuing their work. If this is the case, you will already know some potential members for your workshop.

If you have not had the opportunity to meet fellow writers by taking a creative writing class, contact creative writing professors at a nearby college and ask them to recommend serious writers from their classes. You could also place flyers in the English Department.

How Many Is the "Write" Number?

Workshops can consist of almost any size but it can be difficult to be productive if the group is too large. An optimum group consists of six to eight participants, which allows for one or two not being able to make it to every workshop. A commitment to regular attendance is a must for participants because absence in person is also absence in feedback, a vital contribution of every member.

If you have a huge interest, take names and contact information in case someone drops out but don't jeopardize the success of the group by accepting anyone and everyone. It's okay to have standards about commitment and dedication.

Workshop Leadership

The next most important ingredient of a successful poetry workshop is its leader. While it might be possible for some groups to maintain a sense of order and stability without one, a good leader will help keep the workshop rolling by asking leading questions, reminding members of time limitations or "rules" of conduct and by also offering ideas for writing exercises. Where do you find someone to do that? If you are motivated and capable, do it yourself. It's not such a difficult task with only six to eight people to keep track of. Showing up and participating is the first big thing. Members will need one person to turn to for information about workshop meeting times and places and general advice. If actually leading each workshop is not something you want to do all the time, ask members to take turns. Each person will have something unique to offer in that capacity and it will feel as if it is truly a group effort. Don't forget to keep a list of the members with their contact information and give everyone a copy in case someone is ill or the weather is bad and a workshop needs to be cancelled.

Meeting Places

Where does a workshop meet? A central location is a good idea but if your members are scattered, perhaps you could arrange to meet in various places. Campuses or local libraries make great meeting places and often offer private study rooms with a table and chairs and are free. If that's not an option, perhaps someone could host a workshop at their home. Even a quiet restaurant if you can find one could make a good meeting place. Just make sure there is enough room for everyone to be comfortable. If one place doesn't work out, try another. Be flexible until you find what works best. If the location changes often, be prepared to remind people by phone or e-mail each time. Someone will forget if you don't.

Meeting Frequency

When and how often should a writing workshop meet? That is a debatable question and again something that you may need to be flexible about until you find out how the group meshes and works together. A weekly commitment might be too much and not allow for members to get their creative juices flowing enough to create something that often. Every two weeks would probably be better but then again, be flexible and let the group decide. You need to allow for the absence of a member or two each time but you don't want to be missing more than half. Commitment to regular participation should be of major concern when inviting potential members to join your workshop, and it may be necessary to ask someone to drop out so someone else on your waiting list can benefit from the workshop. When to meet depends on the schedules of your members. It is best to meet at the same time when possible and at a time when all or at least the majority of members can make it. Evenings are popular for workshops but consider a Saturday or Sunday afternoon, too, if it will help increase attendance.

Three Rules of Engagement

Once you build your list of members and hash out a date, time and place, you'll be ready to begin workshopping. A writing workshop can be fun and productive for everyone involved if a few simple rules are kept in mind.

Be Prepared

First, members should come prepared and make sure they have enough copies of their work for everyone plus a couple extra. If you write short poems or flash fiction, put them all on the same page but keep it to no more than two or three pages. If you write epic poems, longer short stories or even novels, consider sharing only a chapter or segments of two to three pages at a time. Please collate and staple pages so members don't have to figure out the order. And if they are very long, consider having members take them home to read and critique at the next workshop. Shorter poems can be read and digested fairly quickly but longer ones will get a better critique if members have time to mull them over at their leisure. In this case, either bring something short for that workshop or just stay and critique others' work. After all, you will want them to give your work a fair shake so don't show up, drop off your Homerian-sized epic and leave because you don't have anything to be workshopped that session.

Offer Fair Criticism

This brings us to a second and very important rule. Every member should offer worthwhile criticism if they want others to offer their fair assessments. Noncommittal comments such as "It's nice" or "I like it" or "Good job" are not acceptable comments in a writing workshop unless they are accompanied by reasons for those comments. Why is a poem/story nice and why do you like it or think it's a good job? It is also just as important to be able to say that you do not like something or think it is good. Again, such comments must be accompanied by why. In addition to why, comments that include constructive suggestions for improvement and revision, even if the work is good, come from the best kind of workshop member.

Keep It Zipped

Another rule of common courtesy during workshopping is that the poet/author must remain silent during criticism of his/her work until the group is done before asking for specific suggestions. Often, any questions the member may have might be answered by then. And, it is important for the group to interpret the work in their own way without the writer giving away its personal or literal meaning or significance right away. Many times, group members will view something from an entirely different perspective than the writer intended. This can be good or bad but never boring.

Cooperative Leadership

What if you are the leader? How do you "lead?" There are many ways to conduct a workshop but it's best not to appear as if you are the "teacher" or as if you know everything. Ask others for input and ideas, or take turns leading the workshop on various occasions. A workshop leader is a moderator, keeping people on track. A leader prompts members to offer criticism with leading questions such as "Mary, what do you think about the recurring references to the color white (or black or purple) in this story?" or "Carl, in your opinion, how does the form (sonnet, syllabic, etc.) help or hinder this poem?" Leaders encourage participants to be specific and don't allow those noncommittal comments mentioned previously.

A helpful practice in a workshop is to also ask members to share whatever they think might benefit the group that is writing related, whether it is a favorite poem, a copy of an article from a magazine, a writing exercise or a tip about a poetry or writing contest.

Time Frame Considerations

How long should a workshop session last? It's better to meet less frequently and allow for longer sessions, so more work can be accomplished. A four-member group can easily use a couple of hour's workshopping which is not always just criticizing each other's work. This is also a time for reading, sharing ideas and articles, bragging up acceptances and rejections, offering advice and learning some new writing exercises.

Consider that if you allow twenty minutes per person in a group of six, that's two hours total and only involves reading a short poem or story from each member two to three times and allowing for comments from the group. Adjust the meeting time to allow for fifteen to thirty minutes for those extra activities previously mentioned but be flexible to allow for different lengths in the work submitted while still giving everyone an equal and fair time frame for workshopping. Two hours has now turned into two and a half and if you add in visiting, maybe refreshments and general chit chat, your session can easily run into three hours.

Reading Aloud

One important aspect about writing and poetry in particular is that people often forget that poetry is not meant simply to be read in your head. Poetry is meant to be heard as well. How a poem sounds can often make all the difference in its quality and potential to be published. For this reason, reading the submitted poetry aloud in the workshop is a must. Even prose is often written with a cadence and selection of words that enhances it in a way that becomes even more obvious when it is read aloud. I like to have one or even two other members read my work aloud before I read it aloud myself. Hearing how others interpret my work aloud can be the first doorway to opening up my mind to potential revisions. After all, as Lillian Hellman said, "Nothing you write, if you hope to be any good, will ever come out as you first hoped." Hearing your work read aloud allows for that realization.

Reading a Lot

A writer who doesn't read is not a true writer. While workshop members should be doing plenty of reading outside of the workshop, an occasional sample by the poets of yore or contemporary artists can only help members understand the process of writing better and may give them a feel for the genre at which they are most talented and enjoy doing the most. A leader could be responsible for sharing or the entire group could take turns as suggested previously. Don't forget that there are plenty of magazines out there with articles galore about writing and being published. *Poets and Writers* springs to mind as well as *Writer's Digest.* Send for sample copies or look for them in your local library or bookstore and consider subscribing. And then share what you learn from them with your workshop buddies.

After the Workshop

After a workshop has been successful for a period of time, collecting some of the group's favorite and best work into a chapbook might be a satisfying way to fulfill a publishing goal. Perhaps someone in the group might have desktop publishing experience or simply be a creative computer geek and can volunteer to do the grunt work. It doesn't have to be something that goes public but that is produced only for the pleasure of the group so each may have a copy or extra copies to give as gifts to family and friends. The production costs can even be shared.

While often frowned upon in the world of academia, self-publishing a chapbook is a viable option and can often be accomplished at a minimal cost with a local printer who might even help you with layout and graphics. Seeing your name in print is wonderful motivation to keep writing. For students, being involved in such an endeavor may impress potential scholarship committees and garner some educational resources for their efforts.

A great follow-up to a workshop group could be a public reading at a local library, in a high school English class or at open mike night at a local club and if they don't, put one together yourself. All you need is some chutzpah and a microphone.

Workshop Resources

Books

In the Palm of Your Hand—The Poet's Portable Workshop by Steve Kowit

Poetry Speaks: Hear Great Poets Read Their Work from Tennyson to Plath (book and three audio CDs) edited by Elise Paschen and Rebekah Presson Mosby

Magazines

Poets and Writers

Writer's Digest

Online

Poets and Writers (www.pw.org)

The Internet Writing Workshop (www.internetwritingworkshop.org)

Poetry Daily (www.poems.com)

ii

Submitting
Your Work

GLORIA D. HEINEMANN

Edit to Avoid a Half-Baked Story

No writer has a monopoly on the "right" way to put words to paper. There is no simple recipe for creating a well-written piece that grabs an editor's attention and holds a reader's interest. Writing is an individualistic activity, and writers use a variety of strategies to get from first to final draft. Some writers love to write, but hate to edit their work and often leave it to professional editors. Personally, I enjoy both writing and editing and view editing as an intricate part of the writing process. Editing has helped me improve my pieces and grow as a writer. Effective editing for me is the challenging part of writing—the process by which good writing becomes excellent writing.

If a first draft represents a cake's ingredients in the mixing bowl, then editing is, as my mother would say, the hard part, where you carefully mix together the dry and moist ingredients just long enough to ensure a smooth batter. Editing also is the icing applicator and cake decorator—the tool that permits the writer to enhance and finish the product.

When I prepare a first draft, I work in write/edit sequences from day to day. Initially, some writers develop an outline and write from it. Instead, I rehearse mentally some of what I want to say in my piece. I jot down a few ideas on the first page—ideas I want to be sure to include. Then I write a first paragraph and gradually work in the ideas below. I begin each day's writing by editing what I've already written. The process of rereading and editing helps me reconnect with my story and orients me to where I "left off" the previous day. It also jogs my memory so I can expand what I've written by adding more details and anecdotes. Finally, it shows me where to insert dialogue to "show" rather than "tell" my story more effectively to the reader.

Once I have a good first draft, I put it away for several days before I begin final editing. This is analogous to letting the cake cool before removing it from the pan and icing it. Time away from the piece gives me a fresh perspective and helps me evaluate it more objectively. In final editing, I edit the piece once a day until I'm happy with it. At this point, I have two goals: (1) to check the ending to be sure it's as polished as the beginning since I've been editing the beginning on a regular basis and (2) to look at the piece as a whole and ask myself what I can do better to draw the reader into my story. Each day I address a number of questions related to the structure of my piece, how well I've communicated with the reader, how well I've told my story, and whether or not the title works.

With regard to structure, I ask myself:

- Does my piece have a beginning, middle, and ending?
- Does my lead paragraph entice the reader to read more?
- Does my lead paragraph contain one sentence that "sums up" my piece?
- Is there a better first paragraph buried in the piece?
- Does my ending satisfy the reader (e.g., resolve the conflict, evoke surprise, provoke further thought, or with the lead paragraph, frame the piece)?

I assess whether or not I've communicated clearly to the reader throughout the piece:

- Does the piece flow logically?
- Is my factual information accurate?
- Have I used correct spelling, grammar, and punctuation?

- Have I chosen dynamic, action verbs and written in the active voice?
- Is my readability level appropriate for my readership?
- Have I used the same words and verb tense consistently throughout the piece?
- Can I tighten up the piece by deleting unnecessary words, phrases, or paragraphs?

Next, I look more closely at content and story line. I ask:

- Have I created visual scenes for the reader?
- Have I used other sensory images (e.g., taste, touch, smell, and sound) to bring the reader into the scenes and the story?
- If I chose to bend or break some of the rules of good writing, did it "work" in helping me creating a scene or character?
- Can the reader see and identify with my characters?
- Have I created conflict in my story?
- Have I "spelled out" or said too much and left nothing to the reader's imagination?

Finally, I turn to my title. I consider the following:

- Is the title catchy, humorous, and/or intriguing?
- Does the title convey what's in the piece?

All facets of the final editing process need not be solitary. After I've edited the piece myself, I almost always ask another writer, member of my writers' group, and/or my writing instructor to critique it. I listen carefully to the comments and suggestions I receive, and especially take note of similar suggestions from different persons. I ask questions to be sure I understand what my fellow writers and teachers are telling me. While I don't use all the feedbacks I receive, much of it finds its way into and improves my piece.

Occasionally, I run into difficulty when paragraphs and sentences don't fall into place naturally or a particular character just isn't right. Some writers can work out such problems by remaining steadfast at their computers, but such difficulties are an indication to me that I need time away from the piece. Often the solution will come to me while I'm engrossed in some other activity—watching television, reading, or falling asleep at night.

The different strategies a writer uses to overcome writing difficulties and produce the final, finished piece are intriguing. I have attempted to describe some of the process, but I think there's a bit of magic involved as well. It's much like Mom's baking talent. Her cake looks as good as any in the bakery window and tastes even better. So, too, a finished piece, showcased in the appropriate magazine or book, gives delight and satisfaction.

ANN DIXON

going to market

A Guide to Professional Markets for Educators

You've got a great idea for an article or essay to share with other educators. But who wants to publish it and how do you make contact? Avoid wasting your time (and an editor's) by first researching the market. Writer's guidelines will tell you the names of editors, correct addresses, required format, rights purchased, rates of payment, topics of interest, and other vital information.

Many publishers will mail their guidelines if you provide a self-addressed, stamped envelope (SASE). Most post them on their websites, as well. Online guidelines are faster and, in an industry that changes constantly, usually the most up-to-date.

The following list of magazines and journals for educators will help focus your market search. Refer to the websites for more complete information. Examine recent copies of any magazine before submitting, as well.

For information on children's magazine markets, consult a current edition of *Children's Writer's & Illustrator's Market* (www.scbwi.org) or join the *Society of Children's Book Writers and Illustrators* to receive their magazine market survey.

Name: *American School Board Journal*
Address: 1680 Duke Street, Alexandria, VA 22314
Telephone: (703) 838–6739
Website: www.asbj.com
Contact person: Sally Banks Zakariya
Format: Magazine
Audience: School board members, superintendents, and administrators
Number of issues/year: 12
Method of submission: Mail or e-mail
Simultaneous submissions: No
Payment: No information provided
Lead time: Several months
Submission topics/length: Trends and solutions in education, leadership at community and district levels/1250–2500 words

Name: *Book Links: Connecting Books, Libraries, and Classrooms*
Address: 50 East Huron Street, Chicago, IL 60611
Telephone: (312) 280–5718
Website: www.ala.org/BookLinks
Contact person: Laura Tillotson, Editor
Format: Magazine
Audience: Teachers, librarians, parents, and booksellers
Number of issues/year: Bimonthly
Method of submission: Mail or e-mail
Payment: "Small honorarium"
Submission topics/length: Multicultural literature and curricular themes. "Classroom Connections," topic introduction and annotated bibliography/3500 words maximum. "Visual Learning," "Book Strategies," "In the Trenches"

Name: *The Chronicle of Education Higher*
Address: 1255 23rd Street NW, Suite 700, Washington, DC 20037

Telephone: (202) 466–1000
Website: http://chronicle.com
Contact person: See under "Contact Us" at website
Format: Magazine and online
Audience: Academic administrators, faculty members, students, foundation personnel, government officials, and legislators
Number of issues/year: Print, 49. Online, daily
Method of submission: Mail
Payment: Unsolicited, $300/article. Commissioned, $500/article
Submission topics/length: Broad range of interest related to higher education/1000–1600 words

Name: *Coach and Athletic Director*
Address: Scholastic Coach, 557 Broadway, New York, NY 10012
Fax: (212) 343–6376
Website: www.scholastic.com/coach
Contact person: Kevin Newell, Senior Editor
Format: Magazine
Audience: Coaches and athletic directors in high schools, colleges, and non-school athletic programs
Number of issues/year: 10
Method of submission: E-mail. Mail, if diagrams included
Payment: No information provided
Submission topics/length: Sports techniques, administration, physical education, strength and conditioning, injury care and prevention, technology in sports, book reviews, and humor

Name: *Diverse—Issues in Higher Education*
Address: 10520 Warwick Avenue, Suite B-8, Fairfax, VA 22030–3136
Telephone: (800) 783–3199; (703) 385–2981
Website: www.diverseeducation.com
Contact person: Hilary Hurd Anyaso
Format: Newsmagazine
Audience: Educators, administrators, and students in higher education

Number of issues/year: Biweekly
Method of submission: E-mail or by mail on disk
Payment: No information provided
Submission topics/length: "The Last Word," opinions on current issues in higher education/600–800 words. "Diverse Forum," in-depth discussion of problems among underrepresented populations in higher education/800–1000 words. Book reviews/800 words

Name: *Earlychildhood News*
Website: www.earlychildhood.com/index.cfm
Format: Online
Audience: Teachers and parents of young children from infancy to age 8
Number of issues/year: 6
Method of submission: E-mail at "Submit an Article" under "Share Your Ideas"
Payment: None
Submission topics/length: Activities, health, behavior, safety, and other developmentally appropriate subjects

Name: *Education Week*
Address: Commentary, *Education Week,* 6935 Arlington Road, Suite 100, Bethesda, MD 20814
Telephone: (800) 346–1834
Website: www.edweek.org/ew/index.html
Contact person: See staff listing
Format: Newspaper and/or online
Audience: K–12 educators, administrators, policymakers, lawmakers, scholars, government officials, business leaders, parents, and community advocates
Number of issues/year: 44
Method of submission: Mail or e-mail
Payment: Yes, but amount not specified
Submission topics/length: Opinion essays on educational topics/maximum 1500 words

Name: *Educators'eZine*
Address: gwensol@earthlink.net
Website: www.techlearning.com/content/working
Contact person: Gwen Solomon, Director
Format: Online
Audience: Teachers, library/media specialists, technology coordinators, and administrators
Number of issues/year: 12
Method of submission: E-mail
Payment: Three-month subscription, free software
Submission topics/length: K–12 educational technology/length as needed

Name: *English Journal* (See "Call for Manuscripts" at http://www.ncte.org/pubs/publish/journals and guidelines for other NCTE journals.)
Address: English Department, 1773 Campus Delivery, Colorado State University, Fort Collins, CO 80523–1773
Telephone: (970) 491–6417
Website: www.ncte.org/pubs/journals/ej
Contact person: Louann Reid, Editor
Format: Refereed magazine
Audience: Members of the Secondary Section of the National Council of Teachers of English, secondary teachers, supervisors, and teacher educators
Number of issues/year: 6
Method of submission: Mail. Include paper copy and disk copy
Simultaneous submissions: No
Payment: None
Submission topics/length: All aspects of teaching English language arts in secondary schools. See list of Themed Issues. Features/2500–3750 words. "Snapshots" and "Speaking My Mind"/1000–1500 words. "Teacher to Teacher"/300 words. See individual editors for columns, reviews, and poetry

Name: *ESL Magazine*
Address: Modern English Publishing, 211 E. Ontario Street,

Suite 1800, Chicago, IL 60611
Telephone: (312) 283–3756
Website: www.eslmag.com
Format: Magazine
Audience: Instructors of English as a second or foreign language, at all levels, within the United States and abroad
Number of issues/year: Bimonthly
Method of submission: E-mail
Payment: Yes, but amount not specified
Submission topics/length: All aspects of ESL/EFL instruction. Theory or research must focus on application/2400–3200 words

Name: *Instructor*
Address: P.O. Box 713, New York, NY 10013
Telephone: (212) 343–6100
Website: www.teacher.scholastic.com/products/instructor
Contact person: Bernadette Grey, Editor. Jennifer Prescott, Managing Editor
Format: Magazine
Audience: K–8 teachers
Number of issues/year: 8
Method of submission: Mail
Payment: No information provided
Lead time: Four months. Seasonal material, 6 months
Submission topics/length: Features on educational practice, trends, issues, professional development, in-depth lesson plans/800–1200 words. Activities & Classroom Tips/250 words. Theme Units/400–800 words. Personal essays about teaching experiences/400–500 words

Name: *The Mailbox* (See also *Bookbag* and *MBX Books* on website.)
Address: The Education Center, Inc., P.O. Box 9753, Greensboro, NC 27429–0753
Telephone: (877) 696–0825
Website: www.theeducationcenter.com/cgi-bin/tec/guest.jsp
Contact person: By e-mail, various (See under "Submit an Idea" at website.) By mail, Hope Rodgers

Format: Magazine
Audience: Teachers, preschool through grade 6
Number of issues/year: 6
Method of submission: Mail or e-mail
Simultaneous submissions: No
Payment: $20 gift certificate for online store
Lead time: Varies. See guidelines for topic deadlines
Submission topics/length: Holidays, special days, curriculum ideas. See also regular departments

Name: *Multicultural Review*
Address: 6 Birch Hill Road, Ballston Lake, NY 12019
Telephone: (800) 600–4364
Website: www.mcreview.com
Contact person: Lyn Miller-Lachmann, Editor-in-Chief
Format: Peer-reviewed magazine
Audience: Educators and librarians, all levels
Number of issues/year: 4
Method of submission: Mail, paper copy and disk copy
Payment: By agreement with Editor-in-Chief
Lead time: Four months
Submission topics/length: Multicultural issues, bibliographies, ethnographies, non-profit resources, and practical aspects of teaching and librarianship/2000–6000 words

Name: *Our Children*
Address: National PTA, 541 North Fairbanks Court, Suite 1300, Chicago, IL 60611–3396
Website: www.pta.org/pr_our_children_magazine.html
Contact person: Ted Villaire, Editor
Format: Magazine
Audience: Parents, teachers, and administrators
Number of issues/year: 5
Method of submission: E-mail
Payment: No
Submission topics/length: Informative and practical articles on issues pertaining to children's health, education, and welfare

Name: *The Reading Teacher* (See also *Journal of Adolescent and Adult Literacy* [JAAL] at www.reading.org/publications/for_authors/rt_jaal.html and *Reading Research Quarterly* at www.reading.org/publications/for_authors/rrq.html.)

Address: 800 Barksdale Road, P.O. Box 8139, Newark, DE 19714–8139

Website: http://www.reading.org/publications/journals/rt/index.html

Format: Peer-reviewed magazine

Audience: Literacy educators of students to age 12

Number of issues/year: 8

Method of submission: E-mail

Payment: No information provided

Submission topics/length: Articles related to the practice, theory, and research of literacy education/6000 words maximum. *The Reading Teacher:* "Teaching Tips"/6 pages, double spaced, maximum. Annotated topic bibliographies/500 words. Include abstract/200 words. *JAAL:* "First Person"/1500–2500 words

Name: *Reading Today*

Address: 800 Barksdale Road, P.O. Box 8139, Newark, DE 19714–8139

Telephone: (302) 731–1600, Ext: 250

Website: www.reading.org/publications/reading_today/index.html

Contact person: John Micklos Jr., Editor-in-Chief

Format: Newspaper

Audience: Educators. Free to members of the International Reading Association

Number of issues/year: Bimonthly

Method of submission: Mail query, bio, and clips with SASE

Payment: $0.10–0.30/word

Lead time: Six months

Submission topics/length: Reading, reading education, and Association activities/300–1000 words

Name: *Rethinking Schools*

Address: 1001 E. Keefe Avenue, Milwaukee, WI 53212

Telephone: (800) 669–4192; (414) 964–9646
Website: www.rethinkingschools.org
Contact person: Catherine Capellaro, Managing Editor
Format: Online
Audience: Teachers, parents, and others interested in reforming elementary and secondary school education
Number of issues/year: 4
Method of submission: Mail or e-mail
Payment: No information presented
Submission topics/length: Essays on current topics on educational policy, theory, and practice; reviews/600–2000 words. Classroom tips, ideas for implementing equity and social justice in the classroom, personal experience/200–1500 words

Name: *SchoolArts*
Address: 2223 Parkside Drive, Denton, TX 76201
Telephone: (800) 533–2847; (508) 754–7201
Website: www.davis-art.com/Portal/SchoolArts/Sadefault.aspx
Contact person: Nancy Walkup, Editor
Format: Magazine
Audience: Art educators
Number of issues/year: 9
Method of submission: Mail, paper copy and disk copy. E-mail
Payment: No information provided
Submission topics/length: Lessons, techniques, technology, organization, teaching issues, and more related to art education/300–1000 words

Name: *School Library Journal*
Address: 360 Park Avenue S, New York, NY 10010–1710
Telephone: (646) 746–6759
Website: www.schoollibraryjournal.com
Contact person: "What Works" to Debra Lau Whelan, Senior news and Features Editor. "Up for Discussion" to Luann Toth, Senior Book Review Editor. Rick Margolis, News and Features Editor
Format: Magazine and online
Audience: Youth librarians in schools and public libraries

Number of issues/year: 12
Method of submission: E-mail or mail
Payment: $175–300
Submission topics/length: Features on collaboration, leadership, youth librarianship/1500–2500 words. "Up for Discussion," column on book selection/1800 words. "What Works," successful library programs/850 words. "Make Your Point," opinions on library issues/850 words. "Educator's Resource Kit," strategies and resources for school librarians/1500 words. "Learning Quarterly," strategies and solutions for controversial issues

Name: *Teacher Magazine*
Address: 6935 Arlington Road, Suite 100, Bethesda, MD 20814–5233
Telephone: (301) 280–3100
Website: www.edweek.org/tm/index.html
Contact person: Comment Editor
Format: Magazine
Audience: K–12 teachers
Number of issues/year: 6
Method of submission: Mail
Payment: Yes, but amount not specified
Submission topics/length: "Viewpoint," opinion essays on issues of interest to classroom teachers/1200 words maximum. "First Person," meaningful, school-related personal experience/1200 words maximum

Name: *Teacher Librarian*
Address: 15200 NBN Way, Blue Ridge Summit, PA 17214
Telephone: (717) 794–3800, Ext: 3597
Website: www.teacherlibrarian.com
Contact person: Kim Tabor, Managing Editor
Format: Magazine
Audience: School librarians
Number of issues/year: 5
Method of submission: E-mail to admin@teacherlibrarian.com
Payment: Yes, but amount not specified
Submission topics/length: Articles on media center manage-

ment, information technology, books, and other topics related to school libraries/15 double-spaced pages maximum. Include 100–200 words abstract and word count

Name: *Teach Pre K–8*
Address: 40 Richards Avenue, Norwalk, CT 06854
Telephone: (800) 249–9363
Website: www.teachingk-8.com
Contact person: Katherine Pierpont, Senior Editor
Format: Magazine
Audience: Teachers of preschool–grade 8 students
Number of issues/year: 8
Method of submission: Mail. Include SASE. Complete manuscripts only
Simultaneous submissions: No
Payment: "Modest"
Submission topics/length: Classroom-tested ideas, techniques, projects, and programs for pre–8 teachers/900 words maximum

Name: *Technology & Learning*
Address: 600 Harrison Street, San Francisco, CA 94107
Telephone: (415) 947–6760
Website: www.techlearning.com
Contact person: Susan McLester, Editor-in-Chief. Amy Poftak, Executive Editor. Mark Smith, Managing Editor
Format: Magazine
Audience: K–12 teachers, technology coordinators, and administrators
Number of issues/year: 11
Method of submission: Mail or e-mail to techlearning_editors@cmp.com
Payment: Varies. Features $400+
Submission topics/length: General interest features/1200–2500 words. Software evaluations

Name: *T.H.E. Journal*
Address: 17501 East 17th Street, Suite 230, Tustin, CA 92780
Telephone: (714) 730–4011

Website: www.thejournal.com

Contact person: Wendy LaDuke (714) 730-4011, ext. 13

Format: Magazine and online

Audience: K–12 administrators, technologists, and educators

Number of issues/year: 12

Method of submission: E-mail

Payment: No information provided

Lead time: Three months for articles

Submission topics/length: Articles and opinions on educational technology. Interviews with leaders and managers. Case studies

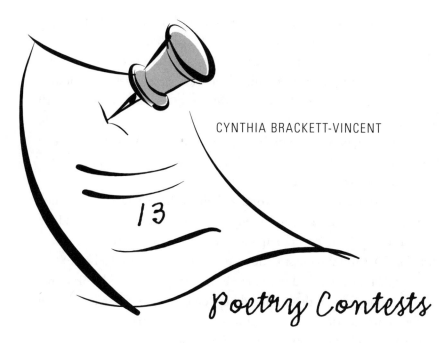

CYNTHIA BRACKETT-VINCENT

13

Poetry Contests

Avoid These Pitfalls!

Back when I was an English Composition student, many of us freshmen were aspiring poets. Our instructor handed out an intriguing flier that promised thousands of dollars in prizes in a poetry competition. Imagine the excitement! Unfortunately, this "contest" organization managed to prey upon an enthusiastic college instructor's best intentions: to promote her students' work and to give her students self-confidence in their writing. Luckily (for everyone else), I had fallen prey earlier and gave her the heads-up.

Here's what happened to me (and many other poets): I submitted to one of those contests. You've seen their advertisements in national magazines, newspapers and online. I was ecstatic when I received a letter stating that my poem merited publication! My poem was going to be published in a beautiful anthology! And that's the kicker. Every writer's dream is to *see* his or her work in print. In order to see my work in print, I had to order one of these anthologies. A hardcover. A big one. To the tune of approximately $40. (They cost more now.)

Make no mistake. These companies spend big bucks on advertising to poets *who want to see their work in print, who want and need positive affirmation.* But they are really, in fact, in the business of selling expensive anthologies *to unsuspecting poets.* Anthologies, among other things. For only twenty or so dollars more, I could receive a plaque (with my name on it!) honoring my accomplishment. And if I spent even more money, I could attend a reading of works published in this anthology! As well, if I wanted a bio in the anthology, that would cost more. (Naturally, I wouldn't want to be the only one with no bio . . .)

That's when I began to wonder. I did a little research and then promptly wrote to this company, asking them *not to publish* my poem. I have no idea if they honored my request, because I never ordered the pricey anthology. When listing past publications, this is one place I'd be hesitant to admit I'd been published in (or, more accurately, been hoodwinked by). The only consolation is that I learned early on in my poetry career to watch out for companies that try to lure unwitting poets. As matter of fact, in the early days of publishing my poetry journal, *The Aurorean,* one poet from New York City sent me a newspaper expose article on this company. A poet decided to have a little fun and sent the written equivalent of baby babble as an entry into the contest. You guessed, it—the baby babble was worthy of publication, too! For approximately $40 . . . you know the rest. Since then, major media has exposed such companies, including ABC's *20/20.*

There are a small handful of companies perpetrating these shameful scams. They use many names as they advertise, names designed to sound like they have something to do with respected entities. How to recognize them: splashy ads with the promise of huge monetary rewards. Remember: *exponentially more of whatever amounts they award in contest payouts comes back to them from the wallets of aspiring writers.* Before you enter, perform an online search on the organization. Read (and judge) for yourself about the company's reputation and it will be easy to decide what to do. Better yet, throw the ad in the trash and send your poem to a well-respected literary journal.

What about other contests, contests that charge reading fees? It's becoming more and more difficult to find writing contests that do not charge fees. They do exist, though, and can be found through diligent research in such publications as *Poet's Market* and others. What's more important than the question of fees is the reputation of the contest sponsor.

Ask yourself these questions: Is the reading fee outrageous? Is the sponsor in the business of running contests only? (Red flag!) If you don't win, does the reading fee include a copy of the winning publication? A subscription to the journal? Is there a well-respected judge? Has this contest developed high esteem over a period of years? Do you know enough about the sponsoring organization to trust that your entry will be given a fair reading and that your fee will go to a worthy purpose? If you do win, will your entry be published? (Make sure you know what rights you are offering by entering.) Do you admire and respect past winners of this contest?

Many legitimate contests charge fees. Fees go toward time on the part of the contest organizers (taking entries in, screening them, etc.). Fees go to advertise the contests. Fees pay for the winning publication to be printed and mailed. Most often, fees go to pay talented judges. But before you lay out your cash, find out everything you can about the contest, sponsor, previous winners and judges. Be sure the contest is appropriate for your work.

The bottom line is that writing is a labor of love and this is especially true of poetry. Even poets who send out poems faithfully and get published often in respected journals are not going to retire in the lap of luxury for their efforts. They make a few dollars here and there between monetary compensation for publication or from contest wins. More often, though, they are paid in contributors' copies. They then turn around and lay out money on postage to submit more work, and on supporting the small presses by purchasing a subscription or sample copy. They do it out of a love for poetry; they are compelled to read, write and share.

Fortunately, there are more and more watchdog groups and Internet sites out to expose contest scams. Too many writers have been taken. I heartily recommend the article "Are You Being Taken?" in the 2006 edition of *Poet's Market* as a starting point. When it comes to promises of big money, beware. When it comes to expensive entry fees, beware. Err on the side of caution, and you'll be the winner.

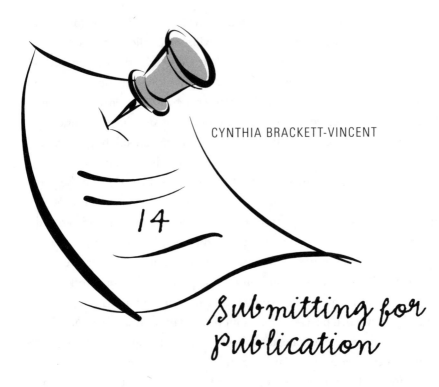

CYNTHIA BRACKETT-VINCENT

14

Submitting for Publication

Dos and Don'ts from an Editor/Poet's Point of View

Remember your parents' admonition, Learn from our mistakes! Like me, you probably thought they knew *nothing!* In hindsight, we know now—our parents were on to some things. As a poet, I *wish* that I had sought out the advice of more experienced poets when I first submitted my work. As an editor, I have the experience to steer you away from the most common mistakes newer submitters make. Here's your chance to learn from others' mistakes with a list of dos and don'ts.

List of Dos from Editor/Poet's Point of View

Do Your Homework

So, you've just finished writing your best poem (or article or short story, or whatever). Should you take a look at one of the directories (such as *Poet's*

Market or *Writer's Market,* jot down the address of your hoped-for market, and whip your creation off in the mail? Absolutely not. Here's what *to* do: make sure you've seen a recent copy of your intended market if it's a journal. Once you see it, take my word for it, you may not *want* your work to appear in such a publication. Is it what you expected from the editor's listing in the directory? Get to a bookstore and peruse books by a particular publisher, if you are marketing a book. Have you checked the publisher's website? Is your work truly a match for that market? If you think it is, take the next step.

Do Request a Copy of Writer's Guidelines

Many directory listings are quite extensive. However, a listing can never completely explain the needs of a particular market. Markets frequently update their guidelines; directories are usually annual. In these guidelines, you'll find special submission information, such as upcoming theme issues (you do not want to submit a sonnet if the upcoming issue is all haiku). As well, very specific deadlines will be listed in writer's guidelines. You may be writing about fall in fall, but the editor may already be reading for a winter issue. Editors frequently express more immediate needs in their writer's guidelines than they do in a yearly listing. Unexpected announcements will be found in guidelines. A press may suspend open submissions temporarily due to illness or backlog. You don't want your manuscript arriving at an unwelcome time. To an editor, the first mark of a professional writer is receiving a request for guidelines. Type a short note stating that you'd like to receive writer's guidelines, and include a self-addressed stamped envelope (SASE) for the editor to send them to you. It's as simple as that and can save you an immeasurable amount of time, postage, and ultimately, regret.

Do Be Professional

Now that you have studied your market and the editor's current needs, it's time for a cover letter to accompany your submission. Keep it short. Make sure you type in a font that is easy to read, on white paper. Include the date, your name, address, telephone number, and e-mail address. Address the letter to the full name of the editor with address—standard business letter format. If you are unsure whether the editor is male or female, don't guess. Use their entire name, first and last. First paragraph: state that you are enclosing your original work (be precise, i.e., what poems you are enclosing) for their consideration in *XYZ* journal (a journal's name is always italicized or underlined, dig out your *MLA* reference manual!). State whether this is a simultaneous submission (out to another market as well) or if any of this work is previously published (if so state that you retain rights). Make sure this market accepts these if either is the case; some will not look at simultaneous submissions, nor do they publish work previously published. Next paragraph: a bit about yourself, perhaps why you enjoy their journal (don't go overboard), a comment about looking forward to hearing from them, then thank them for their time. That's it. You can include a short biography (one paragraph minimum) including education or past publication credits at the bottom of the page, or do so on a separate sheet (do not include your life's story!). Sign the letter. Fold your letter separately; fold your entire submission next (it is time-consuming for an editor to unfold individual poems) with your name and address on every page. Include an SASE for the editor's reply. If you want your submission returned, add the appropriate postage on the SASE; if not, state that your SASE is for reply only. The most common mistake is to omit that all-important SASE.

Do Know about Rights and Copyrights

Before you seal the envelope, make sure you know what rights this market purchases. Do they want the rights to publish your poem one time with no strings attached (referred to as "one time rights"), or do they want to be the first journal in North America to publish it ("first North American Serial rights"), which means it cannot appear anywhere else (in print) in North America until it has appeared there first? Do not lose track of whom you offered what. Do not lose track of which poems you have circulating and which poems have come back (accepted or not). An Excel list (even for the computer-challenged) is a great aid to keeping this all straight. As for copyright, a poet has no need to officially copyright individual poems—it is costly, and we should be so lucky that someone is waiting to steal our poem. The moment we create writing, we own the copyright to it. View the copyright symbol (©) as legal protection only. Go to http://www.copyright.gov/ for further information; click on Copyright Basics, Frequently Asked Questions (FAQs), and Current Fees. A poet will want to copyright a group of poems submitted for book publication, as the writer of a book copyrights the entire book, but *don't* copyright poems or short stories individually.

List of Don'ts from Editor/Poet's Point of View

Speaking of don'ts, here are more.

Don't Send Unclear Correspondence

For example, once in a while I'll receive a book of poems in the mail with no accompanying explanation. I can only assume that it was sent to me personally, not to me, the editor. Problem: I recommend one book of poetry in each of my issues. If the sender intended to submit that book for my consideration for that purpose, I can't guess. Be clear. Or, I may receive a note in the mail thanking me for publishing a poem in an upcoming issue, perhaps with material for that issue. If the sender doesn't mention which issue they are to appear in, I'll have to search through dozens of envelopes being held for future publication. Be specific! Another way to squeeze an editor's busy time is to send a note such as: "Please add this to my submission." Easier said than done. Once again, an editor has to search through piles and piles of recent (or not-so-recent) submissions to facilitate the request. If you must add to or change a submission already sent out, note when you first submitted, enabling the editor to find your original envelope by date. And, include an SASE each time you correspond with an editor for *any* reason.

Don't Bombard an Editor

Call an editor if you must, but ask yourself first if the answer to your question might be found in their directory listings, current guidelines, or on their website. If your question isn't urgent, drop a note with SASE. If a phone call cannot be avoided, begin your conversation with a reference point ("This is Cynthia . . . I'm scheduled to appear in your December issue . . ."). Remember that the editors get bombarded with mail as well. It's better to submit five poems at once (if in line with guidelines) than to mail single poems out to the same editor, one after another. In my case, I acknowledge submissions, so each submission means postage cost, or time spent e-mailing acknowledgments.

Don't Assume Familiarity or Make Inappropriate Requests

Friendships in your publishing network will develop over time. Until this happens, maintain a professional demeanor in correspondence. A friendly attitude is one thing; anything above and beyond that can make an editor feel uncomfortable or worse, threatened. As well, an unusual request is one thing (perhaps you'd like a sentence about your aunt to appear alongside your poem about her, but you're not sure if an editor will accommodate you), but an inappropriate request is another. Examples of inappropriate requests could be: asking for personal information about another writer, asking an editor to recommend other markets for your work, and pressuring an editor to publish you or someone else.

Don't Send Your Manuscript Off in a Hurry

This is the last don't. Review your entire submission, including cover letter. Check spelling (especially of editor's name and market name). Remember SASE. Double-check to see if everything is in order. In my experience judging poetry contests, poets who had everything in order, to a person, turned out better poetry as well. First impressions do count. Now seal it up and cross your fingers! And remember what your mother said: *don't* give up.

ANN RIEDLING

15

Useful Websites and Articles Dealing with Professional Writing

Writing is the craft of placing words on paper to communicate ideas, express thoughts and/or record information. Professional writing entails rules to follow and special formats to use; it involves research and critical analysis. Professional writing is a vital skill that cannot be learned without practice. This chapter will cover two types of professional writing: (1) textbooks and (2) journal articles. Although there are many similarities regarding "how to write" (correct grammar, punctuation, citation usage and so forth—good writing), there are variances in the procedures and effort that lead up to the writing and content of textbooks and journal articles.

Let's begin with journal articles. First and foremost, you *must* review numerous copies of the journal(s) you wish to write for to understand the types of information they are looking for. In addition, it is critical to notice what subjects have previously been written about. Are the topics technical or are they more "casual or hands-on"? Many times, journal will have particular themes for each issue. You will need to discover what these are. In addition, each journal will provide submission guidelines. These can be found on their website. Follow these guidelines closely. (Several websites have been provided below to show examples of journal submission guidelines.) Review their website thoroughly. Should you have any questions, it is better to ask someone at the publishing company than to be incorrect.

Textbooks require much more research. Textbook publishers want "new, fresh and exciting" ideas. It is vital that you review what has been written in your area(s) of expertise. Locate the major textbook publishers in your field. Look at their websites and view all of their textbooks, particularly their more recent texts. Does this publisher appear to have authors write many "how-to" textbooks? Can you find a niche in which no one has written about? Can you find a different slant on an older idea or topic? Think through what you wish to do prior to sending your submission guideline. Who will your audience be—college professors, K–12 students, school librarians, etc.? How long will the textbook be? Will you include a website or a CD? Will charts or graphs be provided? Will you use other peoples' work? (If so, begin your research now!) Will you include webliographies? Will you incorporate scenarios? Will you have examinations, worksheets and so forth for the instructors? As with journals, textbook publishers have submission guidelines. These are located on their websites. Follow these precisely. Again, should you have any questions or concerns, contact the publisher rather than sending in an incorrect or incomplete form. (Several websites have been provided below to demonstrate examples of textbook submission guidelines.)

Useful Websites and Articles Regarding Professional Writing: Textbooks

Neal-Schuman Publishers, Inc.
www.neal-schuman.com/submission.html
This site explains the Submission Guidelines for writing a textbook for Neal-Schuman Publishers, Inc.

Greenwood Publishing Group
www.greenwood.com/author/prospect/school_public_library.asp

This website offers the guidelines for writing a textbook for Greenwood Publishing Group.

McFarland Publishing
www.mcfarlandpub.com/autproposals.html
This site provides Guidelines for Proposals for writing textbooks for McFarland Publishing.

Writing textbooks? Why doesn't it count?
www.psychologicalscience.org/observer/getArticle.cfm?id=1574
This is an interesting article by Roddy Roediger, the President of the American Psychological Society concerning textbook writing.

Useful Websites Concerning Professional Writing: Journal Articles

Teacher Librarian
www.teacherlibrarian.com/about_us/write_calendar.html
This website shows the Editorial Calendar 2004–2005 for the *Teacher Librarian Journal.* This is a good example of writing about special topics according to a journal's specific calendar.

Linworth Publishing
www.linworth.com/writeforus.html
This site offers Article Author Guidelines for writing for the journal *Library Media Connection.*

Voice of Youth Advocates
www.voya.com/Submissions/index.shtml
This website provides Submission Guidelines for writing a journal article for *Voice of Youth Advocates* (*VOYA*).

Instructor Magazine
http://teacher.scholastic.com/products/instructor/write.htm

This website is the *Instructor* Magazine Writer's Guidelines for Teachers of Grades K–8.

Whatever: John Scalzi's Utterly Useless Writing Advise
www.scalzi.com/whatever/003089.html
This humorous site is quite useful regarding advise concerning "good writing"!

Writing Effective Transitions
www.unc.edu/depts/wcweb/handouts/transitions.html
In this crazy, mixed-up, topsy-turvy world of ours, transitions glue our ideas together. This site enlists you in this cause.

Websites and Articles: Writing Regarding Professional Writing

OWL Handouts Listed by Topic
http://owl.english.purdue.edu/handouts/index2.html
This useful website includes topics such as: Effective Writing, Revising, Editing, Proofreading, Research and Documenting Sources, Punctuation, Sentence Construction and much more.

Professional Writing Skills
www.comerfordconsulting.com/writingskills.html
This site provides useful information regarding writing skills and even offers online quizzes.

Professional Writing Style
www.designsensory.com/pws
This is an Internet-based educational component for teaching professional writing style.

Hobbies: Writing—articles, hints and tips for the freelancer and professional
www.essortment.com/in/hobbies.Writing/

This website provides information on topics such as technical skills, writer's block, numerous subtopics under professional writing and general writing tips, ideas and advice.

Welcome to LEO: Literacy Education Online
http://leo.stcloudstate.edu
LEO provides online handouts about a variety of writing topics.

Academic Skills Online
www.canberra.edu.au/studyskills/writing/index.html
This website discusses topics such as: Introductions, Conclusions, Literature Reviews, Acknowledging Sources, Three Grammar Points and much more.

Dumaine, Deborah (2004). Leadership in writing. *Training and Development,* 58(12): 52–54.
This article presents suggestions regarding how a leader can improve his or her writing skills.

Montante, Sarah (2004). Good writers weren't born that way. *Literary Cavalcade,* 56(7): 36–38.
Almost all good writing begins with bad writing—even that of published authors and Pulitzer Prize winners!

Montante, Sarah (2004). Polish your prose. *Literary Cavalcade,* 56(8): 36–38.
The goal of all writing is to communicate, and the ultimate measure of a work is clarity.

Weinberg, Steve (2005). Writers discuss style, voice and what makes for good writing. *Writer,* 118(2): 46–48.

Professional Writing can be fun! You have the knowledge, the expertise—share it. Many times you live and breathe it every day, let the world know your tricks and tips and tools. Don't you always appreciate good advice, something to make your life easier, from someone else in your field?

Professional Writing is not difficult. To me (who lacks creativity), it is much easier than writing a mystery novel! Remember, do your homework before you begin—then do your research while you are writing and always, always, always give credit to those who deserve it (you wouldn't want someone stealing something great that you thought up, would you?). Stick to the Submission Guidelines like glue. Think the questions through thoroughly before answering. Do your really believe you can write 300 pages on your chosen topic? Do you want to write the textbook by yourself or would you like a partner or two? Keep your audience in mind and write to them and them *only!* Charts, graphs, pictures and so forth can often help to explain information—but too many may become boring and redundant. Discuss these with your editor once your proposal has been accepted. Talk to others; share your ideas and get feedback. Don't work in a vacuum. Most of all have a good time. You are creating *your* piece of work, how exciting! You are a Professional Writer, an Author.

VON PITTMAN

16

Your Manuscript

The Nuts and Bolts

You have completed your research, labored over a first draft, and completed three, four, or more subsequent drafts. You have had at least one capable friend or colleague critique your manuscript, then redrafted it again. The time has come to send your work out to be judged, most likely by strangers. In the process, it will have to compete with dozens, or even hundreds, of other manuscripts.

You have long since researched the field; you know which publishers or journals are both appropriate and offer at least a chance of accessibility. Now it is time for the mundane, but critical, process of preparing your manuscript for submission, and then sending it in.

The editors, who will receive your submission, are busy people. For example, if you send your manuscript to a refereed scholarly journal, the editor is probably a professor with perhaps 25% to 50% released time, at best, to devote to the task. While magazine editors and publishing house acquisitions editors usually work full-time, they too are usually swamped with submissions.

Because of the stress caused by a constant flow of manuscripts, they immediately begin to separate the wheat from the chaff as manuscripts arrive. They welcome opportunities to quickly remove inappropriate or amateurish submissions from the stacks on their desks and return them. The best way to ensure that your manuscript makes it past the first screening and moves on to get a fair reading is to prepare it properly.

Proper Address

The first step is to determine the right person and the appropriate office to which to address your manuscript. Both the academic and the commercial publishing realms experience frequent turnover. If a journal or magazine is published only quarterly, or even less frequently, the editor, the name of the office, and in the case of scholarly publications, even the sponsoring institution may have changed.

Most publications now have web pages, which makes keeping track easier. However, not all periodicals keep their web pages up-to-date. I have seen web pages for active journals that haven't been updated for a year or more. Find out when the page was last updated. If the most recent issue of the periodical and the web page are in agreement on all details, you should be in pretty good shape. However, if you have any doubt at all, it would be a good idea to contact the editorial office by telephone or e-mail to determine the editor's name and current address.

Some publications specifically direct authors to address their work to "Editor" or "Acquisitions Editor," rather than to a specific person. If so directed, proceed accordingly. In fact, throughout the submission process, always conform precisely to the directions given by the journal or publishing house.

Style Points

All journals, magazines, and book publishers have style sheets or manuals, with names like Authors' Guidelines. In the case of periodicals, you can find the one for your target publication by:

- Visiting its website.
- Looking in the publication itself. Some journals publish their submission guidelines in the first issue of each volume (year). Others publish it in each issue.
- Contacting the magazine or journal directly and asking for it.

If you are writing a book, you should have received a house style manual when the publisher reacted to your query letter.

Not Closely, Precisely

Follow the specifications of the authors' guidelines literally as you prepare your manuscript. Do not try to improve upon or attempt to justify departing from them. Doing so would be more likely to result in a quick rejection than a request for you to rewrite and resubmit it. A style sheet typically specifies:

- *Page or word count limit:* Inexperienced writers often believe that editors will happily adjust to longer manuscripts when they are exposed to the author's brilliance. This is definitely not the case. Editors work within strict constraints. The cost of publishing extra pages is prohibitive.
- *Citation style:* The guide will specify a citation manual to use as a guide. It will most likely be that of the Modern Language Association (MLA), the American Psychological Association (APA), or *The Chicago Manual of Style.* Some periodicals add wrinkles of their own. Whichever style is specified is definitely not negotiable.
- *Font, pitch, margins, and headings:* Follow the guidelines exactly.
- *Headers and footers:* Again, follow directions exactly. Because most professional journals are sent to two or more readers ("referees") for blind review, they specify that the author's name may appear *only* on the title page.
- *Title page:* Journals vary in their title page directions. For author contact information, provide all items requested, in the order specified. Some journals may ask for a word count or other information on the title page.

- *Abstract:* You may be asked for an abstract. If you should be, conform to the word limit and placement instructions.
- *Illustrations:* Unless you have made other arrangements with the editor, provide camera-ready tables, charts, and other illustrations. In your text, provide a double space between lines before and after a line directing the editor to *Place Table #2 About Here.*

Cover Letter

If you have written an article for a commercial journal or a book, you no doubt wrote a thorough query letter and proposal before you began work, or at least while your project was underway. Therefore, your cover letter should be just a brief letter of transmittal.

For an unsolicited submission to a professional journal, your cover letter should be short and to the point. Explain in just a few sentences what your manuscript is about and why it is appropriate for that particular journal. Thank the editor for his or her attention.

Submission

Final preparations for manuscript submission used to be simple. After printing your manuscript on twenty-pound bond, with one-inch margins, you placed it in an envelope along with a self-addressed, stamped return envelope (SASE) and mailed it. In the past decade, however, the process has changed.

Some refereed journals ask for up to three or four paper copies (hard copies). Others ask only for a computer file on a diskette. Yet others ask for both. In a few cases, I have been asked to submit articles only as e-mail attachments. Some periodicals even specify a particular word-processing program (e.g., MS Word). Send exactly what the publication specifies. Add an SASE if you wish to have the manuscript returned.

Give Your Best

Carefully following all specifications and submitting professionally prepared manuscripts will not assure the acceptance and publication of your manuscript. Only the relevance and importance of your topic, the quality of your research and prose, and the needs of the editor to whom you have sent it will determine that. However, a sloppy, noncompliant submission package will almost certainly result in rejection.

GLORIA NIXON-JOHN

17

Wishing Your Poems Bon Voilier

I had spent years writing then abandoning my poems, writing them then shoving them into a drawer because they never felt finished, never felt good enough. Oddly enough the first poem I had the courage to send out, and was later published, deals with the sense of futility I felt as a poet. It reads:

> *Bon Voilier*
> *The poet puts many things*
> *into the bottle*
> *uncorked and floating*
> *vapour escaping*
> *on some fast brook*
> *or some slow swamp*
> *goes the sanctuary there*
> *A heartsound toll*
> *A seismic hush*

an ocean later
Joie de vivre
untouched.

Not my best work at all, and so very different from my poetry today. Too lyrical and too obvious for the poet I have become. Still, the above poem was published in *English Journal* (a publication of the National Council of Teachers of English) in 1987 and I was pleased that it was. As I reflect on my success in placing this poem, I can tell you that I inadvertently did a few things right. For one, I was very familiar with the *English Journal*. I was teaching high school English at the time and this particular publication kept me abreast of much that was important in the specific field of Secondary English Education. At some point the *English Journal* started to publish poems by teachers, which made me consider placing a poem therein. At the time I was just beginning to write poetry, to take my writing seriously and was obviously struggling with the nature of my desire to write and make sense of why I was so driven to write poetry in particular. I remember something happening in the process of writing that specific poem that gave me a feeling of elevated consciousness, the feeling that I had touched on something profound. And with that feeling came the need to share that feeling. The poem didn't satisfy all of the questions I was asking about my desire to write poetry, but it did address the feeling of futility the poet has in a world that seems unwilling to take the time to find meaning in poetry. What I did hit on that led to the success in placing this poem was finding the right publication and providing the editor with a topic that was relevant for her audience—teachers who were either writing poetry themselves or watching their students struggle with reading and writing poetry.

Since the time this poem was published, I have had some success finding my audience and placing other poems. Most of my poems have found their way into small presses and university publications. But, I don't send poems out until I have read the publication to which I am submitting the poem. I look to see if I am a good fit. I don't waste the stamp if the publication is publishing mostly poems by very young poets writing about sexual angst and such (not to say there is anything wrong with doing so . . . it is just not where I am in my life), I am not very experimental in style either. My writing is contemporary, has become more narrative less lyrical, but it is not wildly abstract. So, I stay away from publications looking for wild, all over the page, or feral.

More often than not I am encouraged to submit my poetry to contests offered mostly by small or university presses. I use two general sources to get me to those contests. One is *Poets and Writers Magazine* because all current reputable contests are featured therein and the editors of *Poets and Writers Magazine* have structured the magazine is such a way that finding the appropriate contest is just a matter of looking over a few pages. Still, I don't submit to a contest I find in *Poets and Writers Magazine* until I take a look at a recent edition of the publication offering the prize. I also do an Internet search for contests. But, I pick these carefully as well. There are contests out there that ask poets to pay a fee well beyond the usual entry fee. Anything more than $15 to $30 for a reading/entry fee should be suspect. There are people out there who will prey on your desire to see your poem in print. Don't fall for it.

When you are not writing, read poetry, good contemporary poetry. At first I feared that studying the new young voices would stifle me or make me feel like a dinosaur. But these voices actually freed me up, gave me permission to experiment a bit. There are many anthologies out there that focus specifically on new voices. Get one and cuddle up with it. You might look at David Lehman's *Best American Poetry* series, which showcases 75 poems published in journals from the previous year. You will see some well-known poets there and some new names as well. But, don't forget the very well-known English poets. A good knowledge of English poetry in general is most important. You don't learn about meter and rhythm without looking at the greats. I have taught literature for a number of years and so I am pretty well versed here. But, if you are not, do some homework. If I were to suggest just two poems to start with they would be "Stopping by the Woods on a Snowy Evening" by Robert Frost for a quick course in line breaks, sound, and meter. And, I would insist on "The Fish" by Elizabeth Bishop not just for the metaphors but for the texture synchronized metaphors create. If you have already read these two poems, as I am sure most of you have, read them again but as a poet this time. Mary Oliver's *A Poetry Handbook* serves as my bible for poetry writing. She will send you to many other good classic and contemporary examples. I also revisit *The Triggering Town: Lectures and Essays on Poetry and Writing* by Richard Hugo from time to time. This little book sits right next to the Oliver book on the sacred shelf behind my computer screen.

If you want to take a big poetry plunge you might brave a writing conference. There are many excellent conferences on both the state and national level. *Poets and Writers Magazine* lists these, too. My first plunge was The Aspen Writers' Conference where I was fortunate enough to study with Stephen Dunn, an obscure New Jersey poet then, a Pulitzer Prize-winning poet now. But, prepare yourself if you take this plunge because you will be immersed, challenged, sometimes humbled by the intellectual stimulation and hard work of the gifted teachers and students whom you find there.

Now go bravely. Take this advice of course, but also take these thoughts from Richard Hugo with you; he says, "To write a poem you must have a streak of arrogance . . . by arrogance I mean that when you are writing you must assume that the next thing you put down belongs not for reasons of logic, good sense or narrative development, but because you put it there . . ."

For me the act of writing poetry feels more like art than the other writing I do. Perhaps this is because I feel like I am making more of a leap of faith when I shape words into poetry. And because this form of writing is so clearly more cryptic than much of what I write, not as many people appreciate or understand this form of communication. But I go bravely just the same. Mary Oliver expresses her desire and need to write poetry this way: "Writing a poem . . . is a kind of possible love affair between some thing like the heart and the learned skills of the conscious mind. They make appointments with one another and keep them, and something begins to happen." What happens more often than not is something startling and beautiful and somehow worth the effort.

SANDRA SUNQUIST STANTON

18

Writing for Regional Magazines

Thoughts taking shape on paper always makes them clearer for me. Combining that with my addiction to learning new things and the interviewing skills I honed, through twenty-five years, made writing profiles a logical step for me. *Wisconsin West,* a regional magazine serving northwestern Wisconsin, has taken me in a brand new direction. As always, the more I learn, the more I find out that I need to learn.

Coming from academia, I was convinced that big words with lots of syllables were impressive. Writing simply for elementary school children taught me that less is more. Refining my work into "kid language" using more direct words and phrases actually takes more time and skill, and holds readers' attention more completely. At a writers' conference, Dr. Dennis Hensley said, "I didn't have time to write a short piece so I wrote a long one instead."

Starting Up

The book I wanted to write stayed on the back burner since graduate school, while family and counseling responsibilities consumed my time and energy. Five years ago, after a field trip on spinning wool, I was inspired by Nan Weiler, the gentle, gracious woman who retired from university life to live in the woods on the Chippewa River Flowage with her husband. He built a wonderful building, mostly made of windows, for her to spin wool while soaking up surrounding nature.

As an assignment writer, I've learned a new craft and met some awesome individuals.

As I added to my repertoire, I traded the instant feedback of the classroom for the opportunity to reach broader audiences. Writing's solitary nature took some adjustments, but a flexible schedule allows time with friends who share my passion.

Story Sharing

I was surprised to learn that telling any story isn't enough. The magazine wanted a message their readers could learn from reading it. The theme of Nan's story wrapped around the mental health benefits of a creative life in northern Wisconsin. Writing for *Wisconsin West* with its positive focus is gratifying. Every other month they feature a local individual who has contributed a lifetime of dedication to the area. Profiles of amazing individuals inspire the readers while letting the cover story person know their work has been appreciated. Adding my own photography to each story helps communicate my impressions. My other assignments have included:

- an official Harley Davidson Centennial artist;
- a harp therapist;
- an occupational therapist who set up an A.L.S. Hospice home and support group;
- a children's therapy clinic;
- acupuncture;
- local restaurants.

System Support

For years, my writing was stored in bags, boxes, a two-drawer laundry room file, or spread out on any available table, which often resulted in time and important papers being lost. Our empty nest provided the opportunity to transform a vacant bedroom into a real office. Now I can resume writing whenever time allows and can organize the things I've finished, the ones I'm working on, and potential projects that are still taking shape.

My completed work is in "Success" binders. Each published story has its own tabbed section with page protectors holding the final submitted draft, the printed piece, copies of project photos, notes, and the project's history. When I decide to return to tweak a piece and query it to another publication, it is at my fingertips. The binder is also my portfolio so show another potential market.

While every person has their own style, I am a visual organizer, so color-coded files organize my projects. Red is for my column, blue for educational projects, yellow for the spiritual material, green for financial files, and manila for B.R.A.I.N. (Brain Research Awareness Integration Network) Team projects.

In my idea file, I collect clippings written by others and references supporting my topics while they take shape, incubating until the time is right.

With long time lines, I need to track where I've sent my work. My "Submission Tracker" notes the topic I've written about, the piece's title, publication where I sent it, the editor's name, word count, draft number, date submitted, date published, and payment information—amount, check number, date. When another editor wants a shorter or longer version of the piece, it is in my Published Work file drawer, ready to be tailored for that publication.

Workspace

Having my own permanent space has made all the difference in my focus. I surround myself with the things that inspire my confidence to write. Shelves on my wall hold photos of the people who believe in me, encouraging me to keep writing. Plants and music keep my spirit lifted. My angel serenity fountain keeps me focused on the present moment. My first nationally published story is framed on the wall. Bookshelves and files hold binders, resources, and reference books. A photo of the entire student body from Kunming International Academy in China greets me every day, reminding me of the two months I spent with them. A white dry-erase board above my desk keeps my story maps before me as I move through projects. Under that board are six individual calendar pages to respond at a glance to calls requesting a presentation or project. Windows connect me with the unfolding seasons outdoors bringing natural light.

Business Savvy

Business records are important for credibility. My computer keeps track of my actual work time when I open and close the file. I record the time spent on each project in my planner, highlighting each project in a different color. A journal in my car keeps track of mileage that I summarize in my planner each month for tax purposes.

After writing for a year, a friend encouraged me to, "Show that you take your business seriously so other people will do the same." That meant creating a business name, logo, business cards, letterhead stationery, a website, checking and e-mail accounts, and a promotional flyer. The business e-mail account and checking accounts help keep records clear and separate from my personal ones.

I registered my business at the county Register of Deeds after checking domain names to make sure someone hadn't already taken my business name. Temporary business cards came from my own printer, just to have something to give to other professionals. At a seminar I learned the fine points of establishing a public business image. I'm still researching website services and formulating pieces to include on my own website.

Senior Corps of Retired Executives sponsors entrepreneurial workshops for new business owners across the country. They offer free consultation for preparing a business plan and guidance through the legal types of business organization options available. Putting my business plan together helped me focus on future goals.

Resource

Handbook of Magazine Article Writing. Michelle Ruberg, Writer's Digest, 2005.

Working
with
publishers

VON PITTMAN

19

The Chicago Manual of Style

The Chicago Manual of Style is arguably the most authoritative reference work in the realm of scholarly publishing. It is certainly the most comprehensive. According to tradition, it originated as a single page of typographer's marks a few years after the University of Chicago's founding in 1892. Because the University of Chicago Press was an integral part of the institution, rather than an auxiliary enterprise, it quickly became a power within the world of scholarly publishing. By 1906, the one-page list had grown into an authoritative, detailed, and widely used set of instructions. The University of Chicago Press published it as a guide for scholarly and professional writers, as well as for their in-house editors. Now in its fifteenth edition, *The Chicago Manual of Style* offers wide-ranging directions and advice that extend well beyond citations, references, and copyediting.

If—like most educators—you use social science research methodology, the publications you write for will not refer you to the *Chicago Manual* for directions on referencing and citations. They will almost certainly stipulate the citation style of the *Publication Manual of the American Psychological Association* (*APA Manual*), now in its fifth edition. The style prescribed in this work is called the "author-date system." It functions well as a means of crediting other scholars and sources in the physical, natural, and social sciences. Rather than using footnotes, it is an "in-text" system. While the *Chicago Manual* also offers an author-date citation format, it enjoys much less popularity than the *APA Manual*.

The *Chicago Manual*'s strength is in its "notes and bibliography" system. This type of citation works far better than the author-date system when a substantial number of the sources cited are:

- by anonymous authors,
- issued by institutions,
- from government documents,
- from newspaper clipping files,
- from manuscript collections,
- from other archival holdings.

In the *Chicago Manual* style, a manuscript's author simply uses sequential Arabic numerals to denote passages or quotes that must be credited. Then, he or she composes a complete citation to place at either the bottom of the relevant page (footnote) or at the end of the chapter (endnote).

To provide an example of the advantages of the *Chicago Manual*'s system, citations for letters from one person to another, housed in manuscript collections, become complicated, requiring not only the name of the author and recipient and the date, but also the details of the cataloging system of the archive or library holding the collection. For example, consider the following hypothetical sentence: "Smith and Jones engaged in a bitter exchange over the issue of fiscal policy." Under the *APA Manual*'s system, the citation could read something like (Smith, J. to Jones, J., October 12, 1954; Jones, J. to Smith, J., October 31, 1954. John Jones Papers, Box 1, Folder 4, Special Collections, Warren G. Harding Library, University of Northern South Dakota). Clearly, such a citation interrupts the author's narrative flow. Contrast the interjection of such a citation into a paragraph with the placement of a simple Arabic numeral at the end of the paragraph, with the full citation available at the end of the chapter, should the reader wish to check it. In such a case, the primary advantage of the *Chicago Manual*'s notes and bibliography system is obvious.

It is not surprising that no one universal reference and citation style serves all scholars. The author-date system employed by the *APA Manual,* and as an alternative *Chicago Manual* format, works well when virtually all of the references are to secondary sources, usually scholars whose earlier work will be validated, qualified, or contradicted by the current author's research. The APA in-text system provides an easy and convenient means of identifying other works in the same academic area.

The notes and bibliography system of the *Chicago Manual* serves a different purpose. It tells the reader about both the secondary and the primary sources the author has used as evidence in making his or her arguments. The pertinent page numbers of secondary works and government documents are instantly available. And, most important, the footnote or the endnote numbers do not interrupt the narrative. Readers may quickly check the source of points they consider important or intriguing and ignore those of lesser concern. In short, by employing a system that does not use in-text citations, writers can "commit literature." They are not limited to merely reporting findings. They can tell stories.

While educators almost always write for publications or publishers that stipulate the *APA Manual's* citation style, they can nonetheless profit from keeping a copy of the latest edition of the *Chicago Manual* at hand. First, it is possible that someone who has written widely on a specific topic, such as special education, might wish to write an occasional piece on its history. While he or she would certainly use *APA Manual* citations for conventional education journal submissions, publications that print history articles tend to require Chicago-style citation.

More important, the *Chicago Manual* offers much more than a citation style for conventional sources. The fifteenth edition, in particular, offers extensive treatment of the place of electronic media in academic life. It advises authors and editors on many aspects of publishing in the electronic age, including:

- preparing manuscripts for electronic publishing;
- citing online journals and books and electronic versions of newspapers and magazines;
- copyright implications of electronic publishing.

The *Chicago Manual* covers every step of manuscript revision and correction up through the final publication process. Here you can find the important minutia required to bring a manuscript to the point of publication. It deals with such matters as:

- punctuation marks, including slashes and brackets, as well as commas and periods;
- variant spellings;
- plurals (always a thorny question);
- when to use italics, capitals, and quotation marks;
- capitalization and use of religious terms;
- gender-neutral language;
- military titles and jargon;

and even

- instructions for capitalizing mottoes.

The fifteenth edition also deals with important large issues, like:

- updated instructions for presentation of mathematics;
- an explanation, with glossary, of book design and production processes;
- an entirely new chapter on usage of American English;
- guidelines for working with foreign languages and American Sign Language.

Because the *Chicago Manual* deals with publishing as well as writing, novices who find themselves drafted or "persuaded" to edit or publish professional journals or to perform the editorial work on websites would do well to acquire the fifteenth edition.

The *Chicago Manual*'s major theme is that maximum clarity can best be achieved through striving for consistency. No doubt all style manuals subscribe to this value, but *The Chicago Manual of Style* does so in greatest detail, and in more areas than its competitors. At the same time, it is definitely not a simple compilation of "thou shalts" and "thou shalt nots." Its purpose is to assist writers and editors, not to torture them. This attitude is best summed up in the preface to the fifteenth edition (p. xiii), which quotes directly from the 1906 first edition: "Rules and regulations such as these, in the nature of the case, cannot be endowed with the fixity of rock-ribbed law. They are meant for the average case, and must be applied with a certain degree of elasticity."

The combination of consistency and flexibility has made the *Chicago*

Manual the house-style book in university publications offices, including distance education departments like mine. My department used to offer university and high school correspondence courses; now we offer most of our courses online. All of our course offerings are reading-intensive; many are writing-intensive. We have long used the *Chicago Manual* as our basic guide. The same has been true of the distance education departments I have worked in or headed at three other state universities. No other reference work provides the range of information and assistance and facilitates our emphasis on quality of writing.

The Chicago Manual of Style is now more than a hundred years old, but its editors and the University of Chicago Press continue to do an excellent job of keeping it up-to-date. This ensures its place on the editors' desks in university presses, distance education offices, and other campus publications offices.

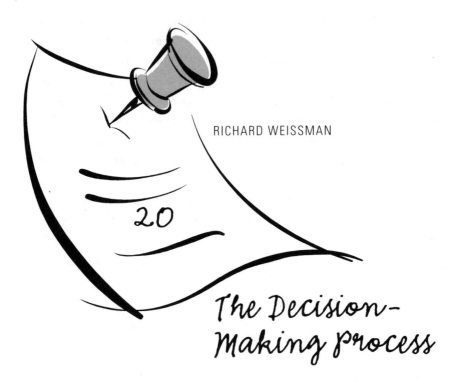

RICHARD WEISSMAN

20

The Decision-Making Process

There are a greater variety of publishing outlets today than ever before, varying from large commercial publishers, medium-sized publishers, regional presses, university presses, subsidy publishers, and the options of doing your own publishing via computer. The author's decision on which direction to go is a function of the writer's analysis of the potential markets for a book together with the question of what contacts the writer has or is able to develop. For an academic writer, subsidy and self-publishing are the least desirable alternatives because the writer loses credibility by not going through some sort of a process where the work gets evaluated in an objective way.

This does not mean that these options are entirely worthless to a prospective writer.

The simple advantage of self-publishing is that the writer gets to supervise every aspect of the production process, from the book's cover to its content. The author also gets to keep all of the proceeds. The difficulty is that the author now has to act like a publisher in order to get the book into bookstores. This can be frustrating and time-consuming, especially for someone with a full-time academic job.

Subsidy publishing means going to a company that essentially is a packager, taking a manuscript and putting a cover on it, and selling the author copies at a relatively low price. Subsidy publishers may also send out some review copies, and even do a bit of advertising. Subsidy publishing is an option for someone who doesn't want the headaches of transforming a manuscript into an actual book. It may be a logical step for someone who is writing an extremely specialized book, or one that is a personal one, a work that is not intended to be a contender in the commercial marketplace, but serving as some sort of personal or family memoir. The author should expect only minimal distribution assistance from a subsidy publisher. The author that chooses a subsidy publisher is implying that her book has a limited market, or that it is something that a "serious" publisher would reject. In other words, many people will not take a book published by a subsidy house seriously.

University press books carry a high level of academic prestige, and will often be reviewed in academic journals. Because of the prestige of the press, and the use of external reviewers, such books are particularly helpful in the quest for tenure. The frustrating aspect of university press books is that they generally carry a low discount rate, which means that bookstores are reluctant to carry them. They also sometimes put out hardback books at extremely high list prices, with the intention of selling the great majority of them to libraries.

There are four sources that distribute over 90% of the books in the United States. They are the giant chain stores Borders and Barnes and Noble, and in the world of independent distributors, Ingram and Baker & Taylor. If your books aren't picked up by these large companies, then the consumer will not see them in bookstores. In the case of Borders and Barnes and Noble, if the buyers don't feel that the books can rapidly turn over from their shelves, then they simply won't carry your book.

For the same reason, they may balk at carrying a book with a high-price tag, knowing that the price is an impediment to mass sales. Although there are a handful of major league bookstores in some cities like The Tattered Cover in Denver or Powells in Portland, independent bookstores are having a difficult time competing with the chain stores, and online retailers like Amazon, all of whom offer discounts.

There are regional presses like Ten Speed Press in the Bay Area that may specialize in specific subject areas. There are dozens of tiny presses that publish poetry, a medium that for the most part has very limited commercial appeal. Medium-sized publishers like Continuum, Da Capo, and Routledge have a reasonable degree of credibility in academic circles, and they tend to like books that appeal to the intelligent reader. Although the large commercial publishers like Random House and Simon and Schuster don't have credibility to academics, they dominate the best-seller lists and sell the lion's share of books in the United States. Many of these companies have multiple imprints, especially Random House, whose companies include Ballantine, Crown, and Fodor Travel Guides, Knopf, Pantheon, and Random House itself. Some of these companies themselves have additional subsidiaries like Crown's Three Rivers Press.

The large commercial publishers do a considerable amount of advertising, distribute hundreds of review copies, and sponsor author tours and appearances. The large publishers also interact with the broadcast media, because an appearance on a show like Oprah's can actually result in the sales of thousands of copies. At these appearances authors read from or discuss their works, answer questions, and autograph their books. Naturally, the more successful appearances are made by celebrity authors, the sort of people that the general public craves to see in a relatively intimate setting.

When a book is accepted the author will work with two key editorial people: the editor and a copy editor. Editors make suggestions as to style and content and correct the most obvious misspellings. Copy editors are like publishing watchdogs. It is their task to vet incorrect spellings, ask the author to check controversial or potentially libelous statements, seek out redundant sentences or paragraphs, and in general make sure that the author has done the most accurate work possible. When the author gets a manuscript back from the copy editor, there are literally dozens of queries, ranging from factual details to grammatical questions. Copy editors cannot be assumed to have a detailed knowledge of your particular academic discipline, so sometimes these queries appear obtuse or absurd to the author. Nevertheless they are in the author's interest, because sometimes the author assumes that the reader has a specific background in an esoteric area of thought. That sort of assumption is what makes books difficult for the reader to understand or enjoy.

The prospective author has a variety of choices to make, including an agent. Ultimately your choice of publishing venue is a function of your own opinion on the market for your book, the extent of your contacts in the publishing industry, and your good or bad fortune in accessing the industry.

For those to whom tenure is the strongest motivation for publishing, choosing a publisher that utilizes external reviewers is a major consideration. An alternative is to publish articles in academic journals that send the articles out for external review. When I came up for tenure, I only had a single refereed chapter in an academically oriented publisher to my credit. At that point, I had several books that had been published by commercial and independent publishers. I received tenure, but was urged to submit publications to more academic presses that used external reviewers.

RICHARD WEISSMAN

21

Finding a Publisher

With and Without an Agent

This chapter covers non-fiction books that I have had experience in writing. If you are writing a work of fiction, many of these suggestions will not apply, because almost invariably the publisher wants to see the entire manuscript. I can think of two exceptions to this "rule." One applies to the superstar author of pop fiction, who is so sought after by the publisher that they option two or three books without even knowing what the author is going to write about. The other situation occurs when an imaginative and enterprising editor finds a short story or novella in a literary magazine, and becomes convinced that the author is so talented that there is little risk on the publisher's part in making an agreement.

My own experience in the world of book publishing is that I have written or co-authored twelve published or about to be published books, and have two others under contract. My first book was essentially an accident. I have a close friend in Denver named Harry Tuft. He had published a farmer's almanac format review of North American folk music, which he decided to turn into a book after a friend of his happened to mention it to an editor at Alfred Knopf. After several months Harry realized he didn't have the time or the desire to concert his concept into a book. He asked me to take the project over, because we had a mutual interest in the subject, and he knew that I had written some music instructional books. Since I felt this project (*The Folk Music Sourcebook*), was too much work for one person, I enlisted Larry Sandberg to share the workload. The book got many favorable reviews in major newspapers and magazines, and eventually won the Deems Taylor ASCAP Music Critics Award. That established my credibility as an author of books about music, and has proved helpful, to this day, almost thirty years later.

I have also written a number of instructional materials for music print publishers. This is a more specialized field, and probably would not be of interest to most of the readers of this book.

All of my books are about music, which is my particular area of expertise. I have dealt with large commercial publishers and small-medium-sized ones as well. On four occasions I have used an agent, but the great majority of my books have come through contacts with editors, or in one case from a recommendation by another author.

Let's discuss some generalities about selling non-fiction books, before dealing with the subject of agents. What a publisher wants to see from a non-fiction writer is a sample chapter or two, a table of contents, a reasonably accurate estimate of the length of the book, and a market analysis of what other books are available that would be generally seen as competitive to your book. Part of the market analysis is a biographic sketch, which explains why you are qualified to write the book. It is also a good idea to include a resume that emphasizes the relationship between your education and teaching and includes any magazine or book credits.

The decision-making process that determines your fate as an author is different with the different sorts of publishers. The work is submitted to an editor, but the way different companies operate varies. The large commercial publishers will go over your proposal and consult with other editors and with people in sales and promotion. If they are seriously interested in your book, there will be some sort of editorial meeting where your editor will advocate for the book, and other editors and sales and promotion personnel will ask questions and state their opinions. Commercial publishers do not usually send out books to external reviewers, partly because they feel they don't need that input, and possibly also because they may feel that external reviewers don't have a handle on whether a book will sell enough to bring in some revenue.

University presses, academically oriented publishers, and textbook publishers will send your book out for review to two different reviewers. It is quite possible that the readers of this chapter have done such reviews. The purpose of this review process is to determine whether the prospective volume is academically valid, and also whether the reviewer feels that they might use the book as a text. Clearly, any book that holds the promise of becoming a textbook can be a valuable addition to the publisher's catalog. If both reviews are favorable, then your book has a good chance of achieving publication. If both reviews are unfavorable, then your book will almost certainly receive a rejection notice. If the reviews are mixed, then the editor may ask you to make some changes in the manuscript and to submit it again after these changes are made. As someone who has participated at both ends of the review process, I can tell you that many academic reviewers take a surprisingly long time to submit their evaluations, and that these reviews vary from useful and intelligent to foolish and perfunctory. The reviews are done anonymously, so you will probably never know who said these things about your pet project.

This brings us to the subject of agents. There are a number of things to consider before engaging an agent in the first place. The first one is that you should understand that the old, traditional 10% fee has now escalated to 15%. Generally, the agent receives your advance and all royalties, and sends you a check for your share, minus the 15% fee. There are a number of reasons to use an agent, and there are also situations where it is not advisable to do so. I will try to explain these varying circumstances, and weave a few of my own experiences into the story.

If you are writing a work of fiction with a high degree of commercial potential, or if you are writing the sort of non-fiction work that will be sold to the general reader, like a self-help book, or a controversial political work, then you may want to engage an agent. The advances given for books vary from absolutely nothing to those in the high five figures. If a bidding war develops between several major publishers for a book, the advance may well spill over into six-figure numbers. An agent will negotiate the maximum advance, the highest percentage of royalties, and if the book is going to come out in separate hard cover and paperback editions, the agent may well negotiate two separate deals. Another positive aspect of working with an agent is that experienced agents have extensive dealings with publishers and editors, know what company likes what sort of book, and have developed a reputation with publishers for representing talented (or hack) writers. A proposal submitted by an agent will very likely get to a higher-quality editor, and will be looked at relatively quickly, compared to one submitted by the author without an agent.

What about the downside of dealing with agents? You may be one of many clients that an agent is juggling, and you may not receive the sort of attention that you *think* you are going to get. In other words, the agent's successful authors' projects may take precedence over your work. Some agents also regard themselves as editors, with or without the actual skills that an editor possesses. They may present you with ideas for re-writes that you find unreasonable or objectionable. In other situations their input may bring necessary clarity to a project. An interesting test of an agent's true belief in your book is how the agent reacts after receiving two or three rejection letters from publishers. If the agent doesn't truly believe in your book, they may well drop the project if a quick sale is not attainable.

My own experience with agents has been checkered. I chose my first agent through personal contact with a person who is a crackerjack salesman, but who had no experience in the book business. The good news was that he got me the deal with a sizeable independent publisher Crown that was later bought by Random House. Twenty-seven years later that book is still in print, in its fourth edition. The bad news is that since my agent had no experience in the book industry, the contract that he accepted had a low royalty rate, which didn't get readjusted for years. Since my friend never had negotiated a book deal before, I can't really blame him for this situation.

My second experience with a book agent resulted in a deal for one book, and another deal that paid an advance but didn't ultimately work out when that particular editor and I disagreed about the direction of the book. Along the way my agent lied to me about her alleged efforts to do a revised edition of the first book, which I was later able to do as a result of my own efforts. A third situation with another agent resulted in that person and I strongly disagreeing on matters of content and style, after some rejection letters and one flurry of interest that did not become successful. My final dealings with an agent occurred when I was asked to substitute in one of a pre-sold series of book, when the original author declined to do the book. In this case, I never chose the agent, but walked into a situation where the agent had made a deal, and the editor of the series asked me to "pinch hit" for the original writer. I should add that the advance that I received for this book is the highest advance payment that I have received for a book so far.

There are a number of things you will want to look at in selecting an agent. The book business is essentially centered in the New York area. Although your agent needn't be in New York, they must have developed contacts with publishers. Despite the wonders of modern technology, you are at a disadvantage if your agent does not have personal contact with the editors to whom she is submitting the work. You also might want to know what authors the agent handles, what publishers have bought work that she has submitted, and whether she has some knowledge about the particular subject area that your book covers.

How did I get my other book deals? By far the most useful contacts that I have developed have come from editors. In several cases I have done several books with the same editor, and sometimes these have been for different publishers when the editor left one firm and went to another one.

The problem for most writers is that they never get to have any real contact with editors. Editors often attend academic conferences, and they are always interested in talking to professors because of the potential of a teacher writing a textbook. To find out about editors or agents, check out the *Writer's Market* and the *Writer's Marketplace*. Be sure to get the current year's edition, and it is an excellent idea never to submit something before phoning or e-mailing in order to make sure that the editor still works at the same company.

To summarize my opinions: if I came up with a project that I thought had great commercial potential, I would almost certainly use an agent. Since the bulk of what I do represents more of a niche market, and I already have some excellent contacts with editors, I would not be apt to use an agent for most of my own work.

SUZANNE L. BUNKERS

22

MLA Style

The Modern Language Association (MLA), founded in 1883 by teachers and scholars, promotes the study and teaching of language and literature. MLA style, which is primarily used in the arts and humanities (e.g., English, history, philosophy, classical studies, and art) and which has been widely adopted by schools, academic departments, and instructors in the United States and abroad, features parenthetical documentation, minimal endnotes, and a streamlined bibliographic citation format. In addition, MLA style offers writers useful guidelines on citing electronic sources (e.g., Internet sites, home pages, articles from online periodicals). As the MLA website states:

> The style recommended by the association for preparing scholarly manuscripts and student research papers concerns itself with the mechanics of writing, such as punctuation, quotation, and documentation of sources. MLA style has been widely adopted by schools, academic departments, and instructors for nearly half a century.

MLA guidelines are also currently used by over 125 scholarly and literary journals, newsletters, and magazines with circulations over one thousand; by hundreds of smaller periodicals; and by many university and commercial presses.

In response to the needs of writers, teachers, students, and scholars, MLA style has changed considerably during the past several decades, and it continues to change. That is why trying to memorize MLA style isn't efficient; it makes more sense to know about several print and online resources available to you; each resource (whether in print or online form) contains useful information for you, if you are using MLA documentation.

Given the advent of electronic and other innovative forms of communication, MLA style has been modernized and streamlined to make for easier reading of scholarly texts; parenthetical (in-text) documentation has replaced the use of footnotes; endnotes are now used infrequently to provide additional information and define terminology used in the body of the text. Titles of books are now italicized rather than underlined. URLs and most recent dates of access are provided for online sources.

The *MLA Style Manual and Guide to Scholarly Publishing* (2nd edn), authored by Joseph Gibaldi, is considered the standard guide for graduate students, teachers, and scholars in the humanities and for professional writers in many fields. This text, available from the MLA, features chapters on fundamentals of writing, the preparation of scholarly manuscripts, theses, and dissertations for traditional publication in hard copy, along with the preparation of manuscripts for electronic publication. In addition, the second edition includes information on the publication process for individuals who wish to publish their articles or books. A newly added chapter focuses on copyright law, the concept of fair use, publishing contract provisions, privacy law, and other legal issues.

One major emphasis in MLA style includes guidelines for citing sources in the text by using parenthetical documentation. A writer uses parenthetical (or in-text) citations to document external sources used within a document, whether the document is in hard copy or online. One exception to this rule is that if an idea or fact cited is considered common knowledge, no parenthetical documentation is necessary. The purpose of parenthetical documentation is to direct readers to the full bibliographic citations listed in the Works Cited, at the end of the document.

An in-text (parenthetical) citation typically includes the author's last name and the specific page number for the information cited. The greatest advantage of using parenthetical documentation is that it allows the writer to present direction quotations, paraphrases, etc., in parentheses at the spots within the essay where this information appears. This citation system streamlines documentation for writers and readers, and it eliminates the need for lengthy series of footnotes featuring the Latin abbreviations, ibid., and op. cit. A writer who uses MLA parenthetical documentation may also use information notes (in the form of endnotes that follow the main text of the essay) to provide additional information that might interrupt the flow of the essay yet is important to include and/or to refer readers to additional sources not discussed in the essay itself.

A second emphasis in MLA style involves guidelines for preparing lists of works cited as well as other kinds of source lists (e.g., primary and secondary works consulted). At the end of an essay, a list of works cited provides publication information about each source which the writer has quoted or paraphrased in the essay; the list is alphabetized by authors' last names (or by titles for works without authors). The works cited list at the end of this essay offers examples.

Diana Hacker's website *Research and Documentation Online* is one of the most reliable World Wide Web resources for individuals interested in learning about the application of MLA Style Guidelines to online sources. Information on this website is based on that which appears in *Research and Documentation in the Electronic Age* (3rd edn), by Diana Hacker.

Purdue University's Online Writing Lab (OWL) is another highly useful online resource for writers who wish to learn and use MLA style. In addition to providing guidelines for citing and formatting a variety of print as well as online sources, OWL offers general information on MLA style templates and sample papers and other citation styles such as the University of Chicago Style and the American Psychological Association (APA) Style.

Today, writers are expected to document their sources as a matter of respect for intellectual property rights. For instance, it is important for writers to cite sources for all direct quotations from a book, article, film, letter, e-mail, lecture, etc. Moreover, it is important for writers to cite sources for short and long passages paraphrased or summarized from these sources. Such a thoughtful and careful approach to attribution and documentation of sources not only reflects respect for intellectual property rights; it also reflects respect for intellectual integrity.

Works Cited

Gibaldi, Joseph (1998). The *MLA Style Manual and Guide to Scholarly Publishing*, 2nd edn. New York: Modern Language Association.

Hacker, Diana (2002). *Research and Documentation in the Electronic Age*, 3rd edn. New York: Bedford/St. Martin's.

Hacker, Diana (2006). *Research and Documentation Online*. <http://www.dianahacker.com/resdoc/index.html> 1 February 2006.

Modern Language Association (2006). <http://www.mla.org/homepage> 1 February 2006.

Purdue University Online Writing Lab (2006). "Using Modern Language Association (MLA) Format." OWL 1995–2004. <http://owl.english.purdue.edu/handouts/research/r_mla.html> 1 February 2006.

PATRICIA A. PARRISH

23

The Publication Style of the American Psychological Association

A Guide for Teachers

Being published takes attention that goes beyond just having a good idea and the content to support your idea. How you present and document your writing is just as important in the publication process as the topic of your writing. Presentation and documentation are called style and in education the preferred approach is that of the American Psychological Association, called APA style for short. This chapter will provide basics of presentation, citations, and references for authors using APA style.

While there are many issues of presentation to be addressed, this chapter will discuss several of the most common concerns found in writing. Namely, I will be discussing the use of quotations and paraphrasing, issues of gender and perspective, and how to include tables and statistics.

Within APA style it is preferable to paraphrase rather than to use a direct quote, unless the actual wording of the quotation is critical to your point.

A good guideline to follow is that there should never be more than two quotations per page of typed print. According to the APA *Publication Manual* (2001), paraphrasing can be either changing the order of words in a sentence or using your own words to relay the message of the original. In either case it is expected that the original author of the work will be credited for the ideas (see below for information on creating citations).

Once the decision is made to include a quotation, it must be properly inserted into the text. For quotes of forty words or less, it is appropriate to incorporate the quotation into the text using double quotation marks around the direct quotation. If some words are omitted from the quotation, it is appropriate to use an ellipsis (. . .) to indicate this (APA, 2001). Words should not be omitted to change the meaning of the quotation or because they are contrary to the point you are trying to make, as this would be unethical practice. Words are omitted only when including them would make the quote very lengthy and when removing them would not detract from the original author's points (APA, 2001). Quotations of more than forty words should be included in a " . . . freestanding block of typewritten lines . . ." (APA, 2001, p. 117). This block should be of the same type style and size as the rest of the paper, but should be indented five spaces. If the lead-in sentence to the quotation is incomplete without the quote, use a colon (:) at the end of the last line before the indented block. The quotation of more than forty words does not require quotation marks (APA, 2001).

The APA *Publication Manual* (2001) also provides information on how to address issues of gender and perspective. This can include the use of first person, the inclusion of information on the gender of an author, and the reference to study participants.

Unlike some style manuals, APA style allows for the use of first person (I and we) in scientific writing. Authors should refer to themselves in the first person, rather than attempting a false objectivity based on the third person (he, she, and they). It is important, however, to avoid the use of first person when making general statements (APA, 2001). For example, it would be inappropriate to say, "we often focus on the strengths of a student"; an appropriate statement would be, "teachers often focus on the strengths of a student."

Avoiding bias of any sort is critical for those writing in the APA style. This includes issues of culture, gender, age, and disability. Many biases are deep seated in cultural beliefs, and authors can inadvertently include biasing statements because of their cultural orientation. It is important to exert a conscious effort not to make statements that compare one culture to another in a way that could imply superiority. Terms that lead to this sort of bias include "mainstream culture" and "culturally deprived" (APA, 2001). These statements should be avoided. Additionally, some readers could add or detract the value of a report based on the author's gender. To avoid biasing readers, APA style advocates using only the first and middle initials along with a last name when referring to researchers and published authors. A connection between gender and age relates to the use of the words *girl, boy, woman,* and *man.* The words *girl* and *boy* refer only to people aged birth to 18. The words *woman* and *man* are considered parallel and refer to those who have reached the age of 18. It is inappropriate to use *lady* in place of *woman* (APA, 2001). It is important to use age-related terms that do not have negative connotations. It is preferable to use the term *older people* rather than *elderly.* The last issue of bias to be addressed here relates to disability. It is expected that authors will use person-first language when referring to those with disabilities. This means referring to students with learning disabilities rather than LD students or the learning disabled. When dealing with issues of bias, it is best to ask for input from the group to whom you are referring. If the participants in your study have a preference for terminology, then it is appropriate to follow it (APA, 2001).

When reporting research results, it is common to use tables, figures, and statistics. APA style provides specific guidelines for including these details. Tables and figures should be numbered consecutively in the order in which they are mentioned in the text, and all must be referenced in the text (APA, 2001). Additionally, each table and figure must be titled. When submitting an article for publication, the tables and figures are not placed within the text. Rather, they are included at the end of the manuscript and a notation is inserted in the text indicating the placement of the table or figure. Generally on a line by itself, the author states <<Insert Table Here>> to indicate the desired placement. This will help a typesetter once your article is accepted for publication (APA, 2001). The APA *Publication Manual* (2001) has very specific expectations for abbreviations to be used when including statistics in a manuscript. If your writing includes inferential statistical analysis, you will need to refer to the manual for specifics. Since many teacher-authors use descriptive statistics, Table 23.1 provides the expected symbols and abbreviations for these data.

Table 23.1: Descriptive Statistics

Abbreviation/symbol	Definition
M	Mean
Mdn	Median
N	Total sample

Source: APA (2001, pp. 141–144).

Another issue addressed by APA style is how to credit a source for the information you are including in your manuscript. This is called citing a source. It is expected that you will credit all information you get from another person's work, whether you quote or paraphrase. APA uses parenthetical citations, meaning the author is credited in the text of your work within parentheses immediately following the information. When paraphrasing, the proper citation includes the author's/authors' last name(s) and the year of publication. When quoting, this citation adds the page number for traditional sources or the paragraph number for online sources (APA, 2001). The citation should not include the title of the work or the first name of any author. If the author is referred to in the text of your article, the parenthetical citation immediately follows the last name and includes only the year of publication for a paraphrase and only the year and page for a direct quote. The text should not include the author's first name or the title of the work. The purpose of a citation is to assist your readers in finding the work in the reference list at the end of your article.

At the end of your manuscript, you will include a reference list of works cited in your text. The reference list does not include any sources that are not cited in your writing. Each reference will include general information, including the author(s), date of publication, title of the work, title of the journal/book in which the article is published, city of publication and publisher. How this information is formatted will depend on the type of publication. Table 23.2 provides sample references for books, chapters in edited books, and journal articles. When creating a reference list for your work, you can use this as a guide.

This chapter has provided an overview of APA expectations in the areas of presentation, citations, and references. These guidelines are an important component of publication; however, as an author you need to recognize that

Table 23.2: Sample References

Book, Single Author

EXAMPLE

Noddings, N. (1984). *Caring: A feminine approach to ethics and moral education.* Berkley, CA: University of California Press.

EXPLANATION

Last name, First initial. (Year of publication). *Title of book in italics.* City of publication, State of publication: Publisher.

Book Chapter in an Edited Book:

EXAMPLE

Colucci, K. (2000). Negative pedagogy. In J.L. Paul & T.J. Smith (Eds.), *Stories out of school: Memories and reflections on care and cruelty in the classroom* (pp. 27–44). Stamford, CT: Ablex.

EXPLANATION

Last name of chapter author, First initial. (Year of publication). Title of chapter. In First and middle initials of book editor, last name of book editor & First and middle initials of other book editor, last name of other book editor (Abbreviation of Editors), *Title of book in italics* (page numbers for cited chapter). City of publication, State of publication: Publisher.

Journal Article

EXAMPLE

Heward, W. L. (2003). Ten faulty notions about teaching and learning that hinder the effectiveness of special education. *Journal of Special Education, 36*(4), 186–205.

EXPLANATION

Last name of author, First and middle initials of author. (Year of publication). Title of article. *Title of journal, volume number*(issue number), pages.

Source: APA (2001).

the APA manual (2001) is superceded by publishers' expectations. If you follow the information on how and when to credit your sources (quotations, paraphrasing, citations, and references) in conjunction with expectations for tables, figures, statistics, and proper language you will create a strong manuscript that will be easily understood and advance your likelihood of becoming a published author.

Reference

American Psychological Association (2001). *Publication Manual of the American Psychological Association,* 5th edn. Washington, DC: American Psychological Association.

CHARLES T. DORRIS

24

The Table of Contents as a Selling Tool

When deciding whether to buy a trade book, many readers peruse not only the dust jacket but also the table of contents (TOC) to get an idea about the book's "story." Thus the trade book's TOC is a selling tool, a different role than in scholarly books. For the TOC to be an effective selling tool, authors must view chapter titles (and book-part titles) with a new perspective.

No longer are titles merely compiled mechanically to create the TOC; they must instead be composed and arranged to clearly tell the book's story in outline form. For example, in one of my projects, the book's major theme was "building customer loyalty," and yet this term was not in any chapter or book-part title, nor in the book's title. That the dust jacket would likely have stated this theme is beside the point. The TOC must convey the book's theme, the "big idea" that distinguishes the book and makes it worth buying and reading. The TOC must also convey the progression of the book's story—chronological, problem-solution, status quo–new way, whatever. The book's story likely has a beginning, middle and end, and this should be reflected in the TOC.

Within these two larger requirements for the TOC, here are three guidelines for composing titles. A title should:

- distinctively describe the material in a chapter or a part of the book;
- use words that will be meaningful to prospective readers;
- reflect the tone of the book.

That titles should describe the chapter's material in a distinctive way seems painfully obvious, but in practice it is an often-violated rule.

One cause of this: failed attempts at catchy or humorous titles. These usually don't describe the material in a distinctive way and may not describe the material in any way at all, but authors feel they make the material appear more accessible, and the book appear more fun and thus more likely to be bought and read. If an author can pull this off, great, but most authors (and most editors, including me) cannot. If we could, we would be working for ad agencies or political consultants, for a great deal more money. And like any kind of humor, readers give attempts at humorous or catchy titles either an A or an F. So if you can't do it well, don't even try. It's far better to play it straight than have chapter titles that not only tell prospective readers nothing about the material, but also may keep them from taking your ideas seriously.

Probably the more common barrier to descriptive titles is generic words. In a book I worked on recently, the author used "framework" and "application" in two chapter titles, and in fact those chapters were about the author's framework and application. But I wish I had a dollar for every chapter title that included these words. The best solution is to use terms that specifically describe the idea, the point of view or whatever you are conveying in the chapter or book part.

Here is an alternative solution to the problem of generic titles. Several years ago, a manuscript had ten chapters, almost all of which had generic titles, such as "Employees" and "Customers" (those words were not part of the title, but were the entire title). I suggested grouping the chapters into three distinct sections and creating three formal parts to the book. One of these parts dealt with the stakeholders of a company, such as the employees and the customers. The title to this part of the book included the term "stakeholder," which created a context so that even the chapters with generic titles ("Employees" and "Customers") now meant something to prospective readers looking at the TOC. It would have been still better if those chapter titles were made less generic, but even as is, they now created an effective TOC. Book-part titles should set up or put in context their chapter titles.

The specificity that I advocate above must, however, be balanced with a second guideline: use words that will register with prospective readers. In one manuscript, several chapter titles referred to the author's problem-solving approach as (let's call it), "The XYZ Model." This would not have meant anything to prospective readers looking at the TOC, and if instead the author had merely referred to it as "The Model," it would have been too generic and just as meaningless.

To balance being specific and using meaningful terms, you can: (1) supplement the title with an explanatory subtitle or (2) use longer titles (these days, some book-part titles seem like short essays). Both of these devices involve an opposite approach from the short catchy titles discussed earlier, but ironically they have the same goal—to intrigue the reader by making the book seem interesting and accessible. Long titles do this by clearly and plainly explaining the book's story, a style suitable to more of us than composing short, pithy phrases.

As for the third guideline, that the tone of the titles be consistent with that of the book, let me give an example. In a project of mine sometime back, the book gave managers practical advice about how to improve operations in one part of a business. The authors had an easy-to-understand writing style that complemented the "how-to" nature of the book. But the titles for the parts of the book read more like an advanced psychology textbook, because the authors used "terms of art" from their teaching and consulting practice. They forgot whom their audience was and were being held captive by their own jargon. The result: titles that were not only inconsistent with the tone of the text, but produced a TOC that gave prospective readers the wrong impression about the book.

The authors cited above could have used subtitles to explain their terms of art, but instead used longer titles with plainer words, which meshed well with the tone of the book. Titles must not only describe the material, but their tone should reflect the book's purpose and readers.

Like anything else, the idea of the TOC as a selling tool can be carried too far. Here is a cautionary tale about just such a case. In the first part of a book, the author critiqued a particular institution, criticizing two aspects of the institution and then showing how it produced several bad results. One chapter was devoted to each of these three elements, and the three chapter titles created a clear and logical flow; they looked great in the TOC. Unfortunately, the third chapter about the results was approximately 125 manuscript pages long.

The author did not want to break up that third chapter because each new chapter would have had a different title, thereby ruining the nice flow in the TOC. This was a valid concern, but was more than offset by the fact that trade books cannot have chapters that long. The solution was to break up the third chapter but with each new chapter having virtually the same title, followed by a subtitle that described the chapter's specific bad result. The similar titles preserved the flow of the story in the TOC, which met the author's need, while the shorter chapters met the reader's need.

Another caution: difficulty in creating titles and the TOC may indicate deeper problems. If an author has difficulty creating descriptive titles or creating a TOC that shows the book's progression, it may mean that the purpose of a chapter or the progression of the book is not clear, or not clear enough. Most of the projects I work on have these problems to some degree, and I urge authors to be open to this possibility. The TOC cannot tell the book's story well if the book itself is not telling its story well. The latter problem must be solved first, because to continue creating titles in that case is like rearranging deck chairs on the *Titanic*.

In conclusion, titles are composed with one eye on the chapter or book-part's story and the other on the book's overall story, a case of looking at the forest and the trees at the same time. Using the three guidelines to compose titles and keeping in mind the need to tell a story, these should help you create a TOC that informs and intrigues the prospective reader, and helps sell your book.

iv

non-book
Writing

SAMUEL TOTTEN

25

The Beauty of Conducting and Publishing Oral Histories

Anyone who is interested in stories, people, history, and/or fascinating and quirky aspects of life should consider conducting and publishing oral histories. All it takes, really, is an inquisitive nature, the willingness to seek out interviewees (which is easier than it sounds), a set of questions one *really* wants to answers, and a tape recorder. The extra boon for educators is that most students find oral histories extremely engaging to listen to and/or read, for oral histories are, unlike many textbooks, "full of voice" and related by people who experienced what they are talking about. In other words, by listening to or reading oral histories students gain a "birds-eye" view of history.

Over the past twenty years, I've conducted approximately 300 oral histories. Among the individuals I've conducted them of are such notables as Buckminister Fuller (the futurist, author, and inventor); Jack Anderson (the investigative reporter); Helen Caldicott (a pediatrician and rabid anti-nuclear activist); and Philip Morrison (an MIT physicist who had served as the chief engineer of the bomb that was dropped on Nagasaki). I have also interviewed a host of folks who are not well known but who had equally, if not more, fascinating stories to tell (e.g., Kanji Kuramoto, a survivor of the atomic bombing of Hiroshima, and Barbara and Earle Reynolds, who sailed their sailboat into the atomic weapons testing zone in the South Pacific to protest the danger of the nuclear arms race, and especially the poisonous and deadly nature of radiation). I published some of the latter oral histories in a book (*Facing the Danger: The Stories of Anti-nuclear Activists*) and in various magazines and journals, including *Southern Exposure, Orange County,* and *Public Citizen.*

Virtually any person who has lived a good amount of time is an ideal candidate for an oral history. Indicative of this are the various topics/themes that noted journalist and oral historian Studs Terkel has conducted oral histories around and then published in books: people's everyday work/jobs (*Working*); individuals' experiences at home and abroad during World War II (*The Good War*); and US citizens' experiences during the Great Depression (*Hard Times*).

Still other oral historians/authors have conducted and published books of fascinating oral histories around such eclectic topics as: the civil rights struggle (*Minds Stayed on Freedom: The Civil Rights Movement in the Rural South: An Oral History* and *Voices of Freedom: An Oral History of the Civil Rights Movement from the 1950s through the 1980s*); the atomic bombings of Hiroshima (*The Children of Hiroshima*); the Vietnam War (*Everything We Had: An Oral History of the Vietnam War by Thirty-Three American Soldiers Who Fought It*); and even a Chinese town in the United States (*Bitter Melon: Stories from the Last Rural Chinese Town in America*).

What follows is succinct in some ways simple but significant advice for those who wish to conduct oral histories for the purpose of publishing them. First, of course, one needs to select a topic that truly interests him/her. Second, one should become as conversant with the topic/issue as possible. That is imperative, for the only way one can conduct a top-notch oral history is to have the requisite knowledge to posit initial questions that are well thought out and penetrating (versus humdrum), and deep enough knowledge to ask solid follow-up questions on the spur of the moment. The need for the latter might result from a respondent not being as forthcoming as he/she could about an issue and/or skipping over one or more important points or events.

Next, one needs to become familiar with "best practices" in regard to conducting an oral history. Such information is easily gleaned from books on the subject and/or by taking a university course or a university-based summer institute (both of which are offered at many major universities across the nation). Such books, courses, and institutes generally introduce students and participants to both the broad and finer details of conducting an oral history. The courses and institutes also generally provide opportunities for participants to conduct an oral history and have it critiqued by the instructor and fellow class members. Learning the difference between the value of asking open versus closed questions, the type of questions that will most likely elicit stories and/or colorful anecdotes versus a single sentence or two, appropriate versus inappropriate times to interject and ask for clarification of a point, and the need to have subjects spell unusual words (which takes the guess work out of transcribing the oral history and also saves the oral historian a great amount of time) are all invaluable to those who harbor hopes of publishing their work.

Locating interviewees can be time-consuming, but those who are determined to find someone to conduct an oral history with will find that their determination and resilience pay off. Among the ways I have located potential interviewees are the following:

1   If I knew the person's name (famous or not), I frequently wrote to the person directly (either to his/her home, but more likely to his/her work place).

2   When I wanted to locate individuals with special knowledge or experience vis-à-vis a specific issue (e.g., activists against the nuclear arms race), I perused popular magazines (e.g., *People, Time, Newsweek*), activist journals (e.g., *Fellowship for Reconciliation, The Progressive, Sojourner*), and scholarly journals (e.g., *Bulletin of Atomic Scientists*) for the names of potential respondents, and then wrote to them.

3   Concomitantly, when trying to track down potential respondents on a particular issue, I've always made a point of contacting those organizations working on the issue and asking for recommendations and contact information.

4   Finally, I also always asked those I've just conducted oral histories of to suggest other potential respondents (as well as their personal addresses, phone numbers, and e-mail addresses).

Prior to conducting an oral history, it is imperative to prepare a strong set of questions. Such questions should be well thought out, clear and unambiguous, and, collectively, comprehensive enough to glean a solid sense of the respondent's life and experiences vis-à-vis the focus of the oral history.

Obtaining the equipment for such a project is a snap. Any type of tape recorder (even the cheapest) will do just fine. The key, though, is to use fairly high-quality and long-playing tapes. It is also a good idea to always have a pad and pen/pencil handy in order to jot down follow-up questions, questions about the spelling of words, etc.

When conducting the oral history, it is imperative to do the following:

1   Explain the focus and purpose of the oral history to the respondent—and in doing so, to be sure to inform him/her that, whenever possible, he/she should provide stories, not single-line answers to the questions.

2   Always double-check the functioning of the recording equipment. There is nothing more aggravating—and in certain cases, devastating—than to have conducted what one believes is an outstanding oral history only to discover that either the volume on the machine was turned so slow that no one can discern what is being said by the respondent or to later discover the batteries were low and thus the voice on the tape is distorted.

3   If one is conducting an oral history with an individual who has an extremely quiet voice, then it is important to periodically make sure that the tape is picking up what is being said. I learned this the hard way. Following a fascinating session with Holocaust survivor and Nobel Laureate Elie Wiesel, I discovered that he had spoken so quietly that all I could make out of his voice was an indecipherable muffled sound.

4   During the course of the oral history, one should not interrupt the respondent in a middle of a statement or story. The key is to wait until the story is completed. Interrupting in the middle of a story is liable to throw the respondent off and/or result in his/her cutting the story short in order to answer a question that may have been answered in the long run, and which certainly could have been posited and answered at the conclusion of the story.

5   At the conclusion of the oral history, the respondent should be asked if there are any other issues, stories, or information he/she wishes

to convey. By asking such a question, one may end up with some remarkable information and/or stories that would have been left unsaid/told.

Transcribing is often the biggest headache of the entire process as it is timeconsuming and tedious. But it is also vital that it be done right. If one has the funds to do so, hiring a professional transcriber is ideal. If one transcribes the oral history him/herself, then it is important to try to get down every word as spoken—including unique pronunciation (e.g., "evah" for ever); slang ("far-out" or "tight" for good or great); grammatical "oddities" (you'ns or y'all or youse); inaccuracies (double negatives, the use of "ain't"); and even off-color words. Some publishers will request that all of the last "be cleaned up," as will some respondents. Personally, though, I find those oral histories that retain the exact way the person speaks all the more fascinating.

Some choose to annotate oral histories, others don't. The main reason for annotating oral histories is to provide the reader with information that he/she may not be familiar with. For example, if a respondent refers to the "Cambodian genocide" but does not discuss it in any detail, the oral historian may wish to note the following in an annotation: the dates of the Cambodian genocide, who the perpetrators were, who the victims were, the killers' purpose behind the killing, the number killed, and possibly the international response to the genocide.

Any oral history that is published needs a solid introduction. While each introduction is unique, the strongest introductions often include the following: the name of the respondent, his/her age, anything notable about him/her, the focus of the oral history, where the oral history was conducted and by whom, the date the oral history was recorded, and anything else that would add to the reader's knowledge about the focus of the oral history.

Prior to publication of a complete oral history, it is wise to allow the respondent to review the transcript in order to correct any misinformation (e.g., dates, names, places, spelling) and/or to clarify any points that are unclear or incomplete. This is a simple but thoughtful courtesy that not all oral historians are inclined to do, but I've found that it is appreciated and also helps to strengthen the final product.

Generally, oral histories are published in one of two ways. Some prefer to write an introduction and follow that with the oral history. Others use oral histories as the basis for an article about someone and then weave excerpts of the oral history throughout the piece. The first format is ideal for books of oral histories. The second format is generally preferred by most magazines and journals.

Finally, an outstanding activity for students is to learn about oral histories and how to conduct them, and then to conduct their own. Indeed, this is a great way to introduce students not only to the beauty of oral histories, but also to some of the many fascinating people within their community. It is also a highly engaging authentic learning task that incorporates reading, writing, speaking, and listening into the curriculum in a powerful manner.

ANN DIXON

26

I Think, Therefore I Write

Educators as Essay Writers

If you've ever written—or even thought about writing—a "Letter to the Editor," consider trying your hand at essays. Many publications, from newspapers to professional journals, are constantly looking for thoughtful personal essays. You'll experience the satisfaction of sharing your ideas on a topic you care about and, quite possibly, write your way into further assignments.

What to Write About: Ideas and Inspiration

Essays tend to fall into three main types: informational, persuasive, and personal. Ideas for topics are as varied as your interests and the world around you. Consider classroom experiences, professional innovations, personal challenges, and hobbies, as well as broader spheres like educational trends, local politics, religious issues, new scientific findings, or social problems as possible sources for creative inspiration.

Inspiration occasionally strikes unbidden—but most often, it is nurtured. Be attentive to the world around you and to your own thoughts and emotions. Learn to cultivate—and record—the ideas that pop, float, creep, or seep into your brain. Sometimes a writing idea begins as a simple phrase, an off-hand remark, an amusing thought, or a news item. The important thing is to write it down—now! Use whatever system suits you to store your ideas: notebooks, file folders, shoeboxes, electronic devices, or any combination thereof.

If you're interested in a general area—say, literacy outreach—try brainstorming a list of specific topics that you either know about or would like to learn about. Then decide whether you want to approach the topic as a primarily informational essay, personal experience, or opinion piece. This decision also determines what type of research, if any, you'll need to conduct.

Beware of a nagging inner voice that says, "But who really cares about your ideas, anyway?" This is the voice of the demon, not the muse! Answer back with your favorite variation of "You might be surprised." Because the chances are good that if a subject interests you enough to write about it, and if you write about it well, your essay *will* interest others.

Writing about a topic forces you to organize and clarify your thoughts and emotions in a way that is not only useful to you, but also to your readers. For example, the 9/11 terrorist attacks occurred shortly after my father's death. Like many others at that time, I was experiencing deep pain and sorrow. I wrote a very personal reflection on grief and forgiveness that helped me sort through my overwhelming emotions, and which, I trust, was helpful to others.

In your quest for inspiration, don't overlook the quotidian or the technical. Avocations, hobbies, and incidents from everyday life can also resonate with readers. I've written about topics as practical as "how to make a hackeysack" and as mundane as the paving of my rural gravel road.

How to Write an Essay: Tips on Process

In general, essays are written to provide information, prove a point, or clarify a topic. They vary tremendously in length, depending on the publication and topic, but often run less than 1500 words and even as few as 200.

Essays have one thing in common: a theme. That's your idea, your point, and your reason for writing. The theme illustrates, expands, or interprets the topic. Every sentence in an essay must explain, clarify, illustrate, or support that theme.

Audience is the final component of your creative mission. Who will read your essay?

Formulating a one-sentence summary that identifies subject, theme, and audience will help focus your writing. For this essay that sentence could be: "Writing essays can be a satisfying way for educators to develop their talents, share their interests, and begin writing for publication."

Early in your writing, it's also a good idea to research potential publishers for their general requirements. Keep in mind that it's often more challenging to write a short piece than a long one.

If you don't have time to start writing immediately, relax. Think about the idea, be on the lookout for related information, and jot down notes until you can sit down to write. But as soon as possible, start writing.

Most writers use some kind of organizing principle. Utilize whatever method works for you: an outline, a diagram, a list, or, as in my case, notes scribbled on multiple scraps of paper. The idea is to break your subject into sub-topics. If you are presenting information, that may mean listing the steps to a process, with one paragraph of explanation per step. For a persuasive essay, note your arguments and then decide whether to begin, or end, with the strongest ones. A personal experience essay may be organized similarly or might flow better as a story with a beginning, middle, and end. If you're not certain where your essay is leading—writing is a creative process, after all—it may help to think of a road map with multiple potential destinations.

Once you start writing, don't worry if the essay mutates before your eyes. Maybe the theme isn't what you first thought, or perhaps you discover a new idea or conclusion. Simply adjust your plan.

Educators face a unique challenge: overcoming the five-paragraph essay paradigm. Please, erase it from the whiteboard of your mind! Concentrate instead on hooking your reader with an interesting opening, developing your theme, creating smooth transitions, using an honest voice, presenting interesting information, and developing thoughtful conclusions.

Some final tips: Ruthlessly cut extraneous verbiage. Use words that carry meaning (watch out for "nice," "thing," "very," and "really"). Consider finding a way to tie your end to your beginning. Proofread, proofread, proofread. When you think you're finished, let the piece sit for a few days. Re-read it aloud and then decide if it's truly ready to appear in print.

Where to Get Published: Researching the Markets

A good place to start is with publications you read for personal or professional interest. Is there a regular opinion column or personal experience section? Is it open to submissions? Often an invitation to submit is found at the bottom of the piece or in the editorial information at the front of the magazine. If not, writer's guidelines are frequently available at a publication's website. If the web guidelines aren't listed on the main page, try looking under general headings such as "About Us" or "Contact Us." (For example, I found the guidelines for *Rethinking Schools Online* under "Who We Are.") You might also try typing "writers guidelines" or "submissions" in the search box.

Guidelines will save you and potential editors a great deal of time, effort, and postage. They tell you what types of essays publishers accept, word lengths, payment, rights purchased, submission format, and whether to send a query first or the completed piece.

Look not only at periodicals you subscribe to, but also at newsletters, e-journals, and other publications you receive. Local, state, and regional groups are often eager to include submissions from their members. Writing for them may not result in payment but it will yield satisfaction, professional recognition, and publishing credits.

Don't overlook online publications as venues to be published, as well as sources of information about markets. The National Education Association (NEA), for example, has numerous publications in both print and online. At their website (www.nea.org) under "NEA Publications" you'll find guidelines for *NEA Thought and Action.* "NEA Voices" publishes practical tips from educators and reprints essays from other sources.

Bylines and credits sometimes provide leads to potential publishers, as well. Recent "Voices" articles reprinted essays from *Rethinking Schools Online* (http://www.rethinkingschools.org) and *The News Review* of Roseburg, Oregon (http://www.oregonnews.com). According to their websites, both publications accept freelance submissions. There you can also study their guidelines, editorial styles, and types of material they publish.

Another place to look is in the venerable *Writer's Market,* which lists hundreds of magazines by type and topic. It includes literary magazines, many of which accept essays, and a substantial listing of contests and awards. Be sure to obtain the most recent edition, or double-check guidelines on publisher websites, because submission requirements change frequently.

Hobby and sports enthusiasts, religious denominations, service organizations, even airline and insurance companies all produce publications. Chances are, at least one reflects your interests—and you never know where a well-received essay may lead. Some years ago, for instance, I submitted a very brief (250 words) essay to *The Lutheran,* my church denomination's national magazine. It was a whimsical piece, born of one of those odd situations parents sometimes find themselves in—in this case, a fund-raiser. I turned the experience into an essay about good deeds versus apathy. The editors liked the piece, so I sent them my 9/11 personal reflection essay. That led to a longer feature essay with photos. A year or so later I received a call from the editor, who by now knew me well enough to trust my work and to remember that I live in Alaska. She asked me to take on a special assignment about climate change that involved traveling to a remote Inupiaq Eskimo community just south of the Arctic Circle. The project paid well and turned out to be fascinating.

So whether your passion is skiing or quilting, genealogy or pedagogy, follow your bliss—and write an essay. It may be the first step on a surprising, and creative, new journey.

LARRY LOEBELL

27

Increasing the Chance That Your New Play Will Be Considered for Production

Let's assume you have finished a new play, that it tells a great story, that it centers on a relevant and exciting conflict, that it has great characters that actors would love to inhabit on stage, and provides great artistic challenges any director would love to undertake. How do you get it produced?

Years ago, novice playwrights had no choice but to make their way to New York to try to ply their trade. There were no regional theaters and very few local playhouses that took any consistent interest in new plays. To make a living, one had to sell a play to a New York producer, see it mounted on Broadway, and then hope that road companies would take it out on tour. The business of theater was centralized, and, if exclusionary, at least understandable. Today, no such clarity exists. Theaters of every size from coast to coast produce new plays. Playwrights have successful careers without ever having plays see the light of a New York stage. Major cities all over the country have robust theater scenes that include and often seek and promote new work by hometown writers. Audiences in Chicago, Cincinnati, Los Angeles, Philadelphia, Minneapolis, and Seattle, as well as many other smaller cities, all see new plays as a regular feature of subscription theater seasons.

But because the theater is no longer a centralized commercial enterprise nationwide (most not-for-profit regional theaters are supported by local corporate, individual, and non-profit or foundation sponsorship—ticket sales making up less than half of the income in most places), opportunities for playwrights numerically have increased while the overall amounts of royalty payments have dropped. Payment to playwrights for production is generally dependent on the potential number of tickets that can be sold. But for many playwrights, unless a play becomes a national hit, plays are licensed for production on a theater by theater basis, in a slow, often unpredictable process.

The economics of today's decentralized theater scene have a bearing on what kind of plays get selected for production. On the positive side, there are theaters devoted to new plays, to risky work, and to finding new voices. Conversely, many more theaters find themselves choosing seasons of well-known titles from writers whose names audiences recognize because they are easier to market. Unlike the movies, which thrive on marketing the new, it has become increasingly difficult to get large audiences to embrace new work in the theater. Paradoxically, where there is an interest in producing new work, there is often no interest in producing plays that have been produced even once before. The result is that new plays that make it into production in one city often have a hard time finding second productions somewhere else. And because the economic risks of producing a new play are high, new plays often feature small casts with unit sets because they are less expensive to produce. Sadly, playwrights are hearing the message. Productions are hard to come by so make your plays small, producible, marketable.

Another way theaters minimize their risks on new plays is that they try them out on audiences in readings and workshops before they fully stage them. Sometimes those workshops are preceded by a few days or a week in a rehearsal hall with the actors and a director and dramaturg. The process of working on a play this way is called development. For playwrights, readings can afford the opportunity to hear a new play in front of an audience, and then re-write with the audience response in mind. The audience gets to hear the words and imagine the stagecraft and theatrical magic, which is often a reasonably satisfying experience. Directors and producers get to test the play, see if it resonates with the people they are ultimately going to have to try to convince to buy tickets to come and see it. There is good and bad in all of these. There are terrific playwrights working today who have had far more readings than productions. This can be frustrating and demoralizing. In contrast, because theaters look to developmental festivals as potential sources of new work, the reputation of a play or a playwright may spread based on a reading or workshop, to any number of places and people that the playwright would have had to approach individually.

For a new playwright seeking to get a play accepted for production, this system of readings and workshops must seem superfluous if not daunting. You write a play, the next step ought to be to see it produced. But the truth is, very few plays are produced that come to theaters as unsolicited submissions from unknown writers. Fewer and fewer theaters even accept such submissions. Most plays come to the attention of theaters from agents, or are solicited after a query letter and sample is sent to the theater, or they have been on the development circuit for a while and the theater has heard of them through the word-of-mouth network of literary managers, dramaturgs, and artistic directors who attend development conferences and festivals. Even if a play is solicited by a theater company, there is a greater likelihood that that play will become part of some sort of in-house development process than that it will go from the page to the stage without any intervening step. At InterAct Theatre Company in Philadelphia where I was a literary manager, we did far more readings than we did productions. I think we were typical of most American theaters that have a commitment to do new plays. We did one to two world premieres per season. We did eight to ten readings. And we generally got over 100 submissions per year. Just on the basis of the numbers alone, production is less than a fifty to one shot.

There are, however, ways to improve your chances of getting your work on stage. While there is a lot of new play production in New York, dreaming of Broadway or off Broadway is probably self-defeating. Look for local opportunities at smaller theaters, and learn what kinds of plays theaters in your area are looking for. Smaller theaters may be more likely to take risks than larger ones. Go to see new plays staged by those companies that do new work in your area. Try to see enough work to get a sense of the esthetic of the company. Introduce yourself to the artistic staff when you go to see their work. Tell the artistic staff you are a playwright and ask if there are opportunities to develop your work with the theater or if they know of any in your area. Buy a copy of the *Dramatists Sourcebook* from Theater Communications

Group, and enter every competition for development or production you can. Plays submitted to contests are often read blind, which means the fact that you have no reputation as a playwright will not hinder you. Try writing short plays, particularly ten-minute plays, as a way to exercise your craft. There are more short play festivals that fully produce the work they accept than there are full-length play festivals or competitions. Getting your plays read and possibly produced in competitive festivals help you build a reputation which will help you open the door at other theaters.

If you are an academic, and many playwrights have attachments to academic institutions, there may be production opportunities within your institution or within organizations your institution already belongs to. There are regional and national theater-in-education conferences at which new plays are read and sometimes produced. And the theater department at your school may have opportunities and interested and trained student actors, technical people, and directors who are eager to try their hand at developing or even producing new work.

But my most important advice is, go to the theater. See as many new and contemporary plays as you can. Learn what plays are making a splash in the contemporary theater and try to figure out how they work stylistically. The best contemporary stage writing exploits the limitations that theater economics impose by doubling parts, subverting realism, and upping the imaginative quotient of the work. While playwriting no longer drives the dominant dramatic form in our culture, it is far richer, more varied, and more imaginative than most film or television writing, in part because there are fewer formal restrictions than there are in film and television. The theatrical imagination is alive and well despite the difficulties theaters sometimes have selling tickets to new plays.

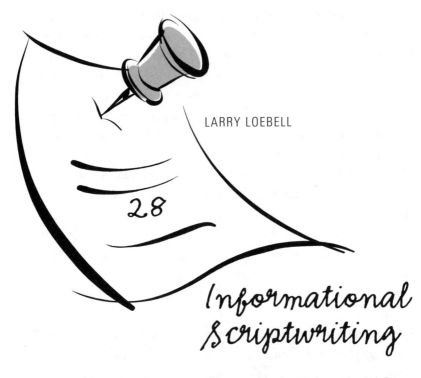

LARRY LOEBELL

28

Informational Scriptwriting

Corporate and Educational Programs and Broadcast Documentaries

When I started working as a television writer, most of my early work was research based. I was working in what was called the non-broadcast market. My first clients were mostly media directors from corporate communication departments. They usually wanted some specific process, sales technique, product, or policy documented or explained, generally for the edification of their own employees. In those days, before web-casts and easily distributed DVDs, most of my work was viewed in conference rooms and cafeterias. My job was to learn everything I needed about the subject, usually by interviewing content experts and/or by doing library research, and then write a script to the client's specifications, translating what I knew into a compelling and producible television program. I wrote on a variety of topics. How to clean and re-stock the fresh fish display, for a national supermarket chain; how to get the maximum growth out of seasonal flowering plants, for a commercial florist; the history of fire insurance; the history of the travel industry; and the history of photography. I also did a lot of writing about total quality assurance and customer service.

Informational scripts really have two readers. The first reader is your client, who wants to be assured that all of the points he needs his audience to understand are included and that everything jibes with the facts. Sometimes the client is a committee. The second reader is the actual director of the piece, who will take that script and use it as a step-by-step blueprint for producing the film or video. There are several standard script formats and individual clients and directors have their preferences. The director takes the writer's words and translates them into the instructions the camera and sound crew need to capture what the writer has called for in the script. Because filming often occurs out of order, describing the visuals in detail in the script enables directors to organize their part of the process.

Most factual material organizes itself in simple ways. Processes have beginnings, middles, and ends. Histories follow chronology. Material that presents options, like videos about complex, multi-faceted historical events, is more difficult. But even complex material can be broken down into significant ideas and supporting ones. Organizing the material is crucial. Early in my career I was given a great piece of advice. A mentor told me to always remember that I was hired to make a *visual* presentation. The visuals needed to be compelling and purposeful on their own. Otherwise I was just writing a radio script illustrated with pictures. It is easy to forget, when confronted with a mountain of information, that what film and video (and now digital media) do best is present and highlight high-level information in association with visual stimuli. The better the visual association, the fewer words of explanation are needed. My job was to find an organizing principle for their material that could be easily and powerfully presented visually.

Later, I began to get more complicated assignments. Educational material that included histories of technology or charted business change. For me, history has always seemed to be essentially storytelling. Who did what when? Often I was able to find characters to tell those stories. I approached the writing of history the same way I approached writing drama (which I was doing at the same time). I tried to find stories that showed how the founders of companies or the inventors of important technology or processes, or the propagators of ideas, struggled to overcome the obstacles to their goals. Audiences—even corporate audiences who are being compelled by corporate policy-makers to watch videos so that they become more informed or more deeply invested employees, crave drama in their storytelling and are used to a story-telling structure that shows heroes overcoming obstacles to reach goals. Using an impersonal narration to tell a story was always less desirable to me than finding a character whose quest to achieve a goal gave the story more immediacy and life. But when I did write voice-over or stand-up narration, I always tried to remember to think dramatically, to tell a story, and to frame that story as if it had important consequences.

Occasionally I was able to convince a client to try something really creative. I wrote a short Broadway-style musical about customer service for one client, a parody of *Ghost Busters* for another, and a dramatic television series about the dangers of bid rigging in closed contract negotiations as ethics training for another. In each of these cases, elaborate sets, professional actors, and production crews with broadcast television or film experience were contracted to give the finished products a similar feel and appeal to their broadcast or theatrical equivalents. These programs were successful because they delivered important ideas as dramatic, visual storytelling in an entertaining way.

When I started to write documentary film scripts about local historical subjects, I discovered that historical documentaries often command smaller production budgets than corporate productions. Historical scenes, re-enacted with compelling visual detail, are expensive to create. As the writer it was my job to understand what everything cost, so that the scripts I wrote were actually producible within the constraints of their budgets. Understanding how production works, what aspects are labor or cost intensive, and how visuals translate into dollars enabled me to write scripts that were not only producible technically but also came in on budget. In the corporate and educational television world, writers who understand production and budget constraints are rewarded with more work. Being asked to work with a limited budget does not necessarily mean reducing the visual panache of the script you are writing. But it does mean thinking creatively about what can be produced for the dollars available.

The context for viewing the programs produced from your scripts may be classrooms, worksites, or living rooms, but in all cases the standards for keeping a viewer's attention are high. Careful research and precise reporting are a crucial part of writing informational material. Strong visuals, powerful drama, and good storytelling help audiences invest in and retain that information.

KATIE MCKY

29

The Keys to Personal Profiles

Want to be published? Then write a profile. Editors need them: lots of them. That's because people like to read about people.

So, how do you pitch a profile? And how do you write a profile that people will pay to read? Well, if Tom Cruise is your pal, it's easy. However, you don't need an ace in the hole to be paid to profile. In poker and in profiles, a pair of 3s beats an ace in the hole.

The Three Keys to Structure

The Hook

A hook begins the profile and a profile's pitch. To write your first profile, you must pitch the person you wish to profile to an editor. A pitch is a 1–3 paragraph proposal. You could call or snailmail an editor, but many editors prefer e-mail. E-mail addresses can be found at a magazine's website or in *Writer's Market*.

To persuade an editor, you must have a hook. A hook compels editors and then readers to care about a stranger. If they care, they'll pay for your profile.

What makes readers care about a stranger? Novelty and achievement do. Anne Morrow Lindbergh wrote: "In the final analysis, we are all alone."

That's true. And most of us are deep navel gazers, immersed in our lives. But we'll read about a stranger's life if their life is drastically different than ours. Such a life gives us a look into something we'll never experience.

Thus, even if we're comfy homebodies, we'll read about a woman who walks across the United States. We'll want to know what life is like on a long, dusty road, even if we don't want to walk that road. To sell such a story, consider a magazine's readership. Is there something congruent about the country-crossing woman and a particular magazine's readership? For example, if the woman is a teacher on sabbatical, then sell her story to one of the many magazines that target teachers.

And you can sell a story more than once. I once sold a story of a Japanese researcher that became a professional cyclist to three magazines: an Asian American magazine, the alumni magazine of her college, and the Rotary's magazine, for they sponsored her when she arrived in America.

Achievement can also sell a story. We all have unrealized dreams, thus we like to read about people that achieve their dreams. Such stories give us hope. Thus, a recent college graduate that opens a coffee shop can appeal to all those with entrepreneurial aspirations.

But whether you focus on novelty, achievement, or both, you must hook the editor in the first sentence of your pitch. If the editor accepts your profile, you must then hook the reader in the first sentence of your piece.

Begin with a cliffhanger and rather than resolve it, back up through the events that led to that precipitous moment in a person's life. Profiling is a bit like a burlesque queen. You only flash something tantalizing. Intrigue hooks.

The Conflict

Ever heard someone tell a story that had no point? Conflict provides the point. Without conflict, you don't have a story worth telling. Only with conflict can you have resolution. So, center your story on conflict. Such conflict-centered stories are cathartic for people. People don't just like to read about people that overcome. Conflict-centered stories give us hope. They also sell.

So, if you hope to be published, don't pitch a story that doesn't contain the requisite conflict. Because life is inherently dramatic, conflict is present in everyone's life. That conflict might be external (such as overcoming racism) or internal (such as overcoming self-doubt).

When you profile a person, you locate the conflict in their story through the interview. Ask questions that surface both internal and external conflict, such as:

"When were you afraid?"

"Did you ever believe you couldn't do it?"

"What was hardest about that time?"

"Did you encounter naysayers?"

Allowing it to get bad in your article also allows it to get better. So, locate the *hard times* in a person's tale. And tell those *hard times*. To a writer, *hard times* are the good stuff.

The Transformation

If *hard times* are the good stuff, then the best stuff is transformation. Transformation can powerfully close a profile. A hook begins a profile, conflict fills the middle, and transformation poignantly ends it. Transformation is the change that occurs in a person as a consequence of overcoming conflict.

Again, the key to revealing transformation is the questions you pose during the interview. Here are some that work well:

"What might you do differently today?"

"After all that happened to you, what's shifted inside of you?"

"What advice do you have for others in a similar situation?"

"What do you love about where you are now?"

Consider closing the profile with the most personal, introspective, and emotive words of your interview. I end many profiles with the words of the person I've profiled. I don't amend those words with subsequent words of my own. If you question well, if you plumb their interior, their words will stand without support.

The Three Key Components

Just the Facts, Ma'am

Facts aren't as sexy as a hook, conflict, and transformation, but they're an essential part of every profile. Facts are names, places, and dates. Procure them even if you believe you might not need them. Some editors want a maximum amount of minutiae. Others settle for lots less.

And fact check. This is easy with the Internet. Don't misspell a college or a hometown. Google and get it right.

The facts are an easy way to begin an interview. Talking to the press induces anxiety in some folks. So, to grease their conversational gears, ask the easy questions first, like:

"Where were you born?"

"Where did you attend school?"

"What did you study?"

"What's your title?"

Once you have your subject talking, you can then surface their conflicts and their transformation.

Put the Reader There

Once your interviewee starts talking, don't always settle for what flows from their spigot.

They might say, because they are humble or shy, "School was hard. Sometimes."

That's too vague for your readers to care.

If they say, "School was hard," then ask, "Can you tell me a story that shows how school was hard?"

The researcher turned cyclist told me that school was sometimes hard. When I prodded her, she told of milking cows and shoveling snow from her roof before going to school. She said that she walked four miles to school and arrived "stinky," smelling of cow dung and hay because there was never time to bathe before her school day.

Those are emotive details and the key to readers caring.

Likewise, when the cyclist alluded to the trials of the road, I asked her to specify. She then talked about relieving herself behind bushes and sleeping in pint-sized Batman beds, for professional women cyclists are thinly financed, and they often sleep in the beds of their fans' children.

Such details reveal more than the look of a person's life. They reveal the passion of the people you profile. And it's easy to be passionate about a person in a profile if their passion is apparent: when the reader sees that they endured deprivations to achieve.

Keep It Simple

Keep your voice simple. A profile isn't the place to display your semantic suppleness. Your job is to tell someone else's story, so don't shift attention to you with fancy prose.

Now, you might want your readers to react, "Wow! This writer is amazing! She could pull any sentence out of her cranium. She could coax words to jump through flaming hoops."

But that's not your job. Your role is to keep your reader tied to the story with taut, simple storytelling.

You might also be tempted to enhance the voice of the person you're profiling. Don't. Generally, you should quote verbatim. You don't want your interviewee sounding like your twin. Then all the words blur. Different styles of expression spice up a profile.

To further spice your profile, consider integrating other voices. This is easy.

Ask your interviewee: "So, who do you know that can talk about your experience?"

Then call those folks and value their voices too: verbatim.

To close your interview, leave it open. Encourage your interviewee to call you or write you if they recall a telling anecdote.

And also ask the two best questions: "Is there a question I didn't ask that you wish I had? And if so, what's the answer?"

This is the place in an interview where your interviewee will often speak to their transformation.

And that's the best stuff.

MAGGIE MIESKE

newsletters in a nutshell

Many businesses, clubs and organizations publish a newsletter for clients or members. Classrooms and schools often publish newsletters with contributions from staff and students both. Who better to call on for such a task than aspiring writers! Editing and writing for a newsletter is a wonderful opportunity to hone writing skills and get a small taste of what it's like from behind the desk of an editor.

Newsletters for Businesses

A few years ago my husband, Nelson, started his own business as a farrier. As the business grew, he found it increasingly difficult to communicate mass information to all of his clients. At first, we started out sending notes and letters. Soon, we had a handful of "ads"—people wanting to buy or sell a horse, a saddle or a service related to horses. We couldn't keep them all straight. Soon, one page became two which became three and before long, Hoofprint Press was born. I wrote most of the articles myself relying on Internet research, books and the personal experiences of my husband and myself.

What Do You Put in a Business Newsletter?

Anything you want to or need to! We included a Farrier's Corner page where clients asked questions and Nelson answered them for the benefit of everyone. We included our current price list for services and any updates related to those services. We addressed hoof care concerns, news releases related to horse health or legislation and other topics that were of importance to horse owners. There was a classified ads page and clients could advertise for free. Eventually, we added a news and notes page that was simply personal information about our clients or ourselves, poetry, anecdotes, brags or boasts, or "in memory of" announcements. We included contact information in every issue as well.

Club Newsletters

A club newsletter will contain information that club members need. While much of a club newsletter may be similar to one you would edit for a business—classifieds, news and notes, contact information (for officers or committees), news releases pertinent to the club or the club's activities, etc.— it will often contain many articles or stories submitted by members. Membership information and forms are also essential in a club newsletter.

If it is a competitive organization, it may contain a calendar of events, results or points standings from competitions. Once a year (Spring issue), the Hoofbeats newsletter that I edit quarterly for Great Lakes Distance Riding Association publishes its by-laws, guidelines, rules and regulations plus criteria for year-end awards.

School Newsletters

A local middle school publishes a newsletter similar to a newspaper in which the students submit articles, stories and even photos, plus sell and prepare ads for local businesses. It's a wonderful effort in which the entire school is involved and I love to read the articles and stories by fledgling adolescent writers. It is these kinds of early writing opportunities that will prepare the authors and poets of tomorrow.

Appearances Count

A newsletter can include any information that you feel is vital to the business, club or school, and can be organized in any way, shape or form. Some are published in two or three columns with a header or logo of some sort on the first page. They can also be published as one page or in blocks and sections much like a newspaper. Don't forget to give your issues a number and identify it by month and year or perhaps by season. Hoofbeats began their newsletter many years ago and have used "volume" to identify the year and "issue" to identify each one as it is published (four times a year).

Another Thing to Think About

I started out using Print Shop Presswriter that is nice for including photos and graphics. I later discovered Microsoft Works has a fairly easy newsletter option and have since graduated to WordPerfect that allows me the additional ability of publishing a newsletter to PDF format, making it very easy to share over the Internet or send by e-mail if it is not a terribly large issue. Another thing that will make life easier for a newsletter editor is to make sure to save previous issues, establishing a format that can serve as a template for the issues that follow.

Best Effort, No Excuses

However you choose to lay out the newsletter, it must appear professional, be neat, clean and concise, and contain no typos. I do not submit my work to publications that are sloppy in proofreading or lax in the quality of the work accepted for publication. Maintain those standards. To the best of your ability, proofread submissions for newsletters and make corrections that do not alter the nature of the author's intentions. If something is terribly bad and needs major revisions, ask the author for permission to assist them in the revision process. You will want any newsletter that you edit, whether it is for yourself as a business endeavor, a club, school or anyone else to be something that you can be proud of.

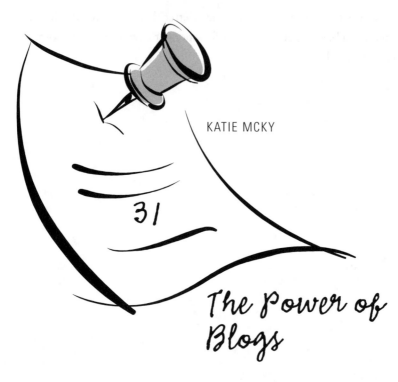

KATIE MCKY

31

The Power of Blogs

Turbo-Charging Your Teaching
. . . and Writing

Without readers, you're a journalist, a diarist: a person that keeps their words in a bed stand. Now, private words are fine. A journal serves many purposes. But a private, daily log of your life separates you from feedback—and critique can transform. A Web log, or a blog, is a public journal: a journal that is read around the world. This global publication is powerful.

"When you're writing in public," says Rebecca Blood, "the minute you get that first comment or e-mail, it sharpens you up tremendously. You'll have no idea of the difference you'll incur until it happens."

Blood (www.rebeccablood.net) is a pioneer blogger.

"I was the sixth woman in the world by my count," the San Franciscan says. "There were about fifty altogether, men and women, when I began. I thought I was late in the game. I was a little embarrassed."

Since Blood began, about 26,000,000 bloggers have joined her. Being timely, articulate, and plucky, Blood has made a profession of blogging. The author of *The Weblog Handbook: Practical Advice on Creating and Maintaining Your Blog,* Blood, now travels the country. She speaks about blogging—and what it's taught her about writing.

"Every writing course," she says, "that I've ever taken and every writing book that I've ever read says: 'Write everyday.' I would never have done that without a blog. I've seen people progress from being mediocre writers to quite good just by blogging."

Zane Safrit (www.zane.typepad.com), 51, the CEO of Conference Calls Unlimited, agrees: "It's a powerful way to improve your writing skills. There's nothing better than writing daily to improve your writing."

Blood and Safrit incorporate links in their blogs. Links are *hyperlinks,* which, at the click of the mouse, transport a reader to another site in the Web.

"I blog to share information," says Blood. "I post interesting links that I find, which lead my readers to intriguing stories and other bloggers. I provide a filtering function for my readers by pre-surfing the web. My linking-style is in the minority, but it's vastly underrated. My favorite blogs are still the link-driven blogs. I call it targeted serendipity."

Rather than write at length about a topic, Blood and Safrit lead their readers to what others have written—and provide pithy commentary. Safrit and Blood also expound the reach of their blogs.

"It expands my world," says Safrit. "Blogging is the most efficient social networking resource in the world. You can speak in your voice at your leisure, schedule, and pace. You can discuss with the entire world your thoughts on any subject—and your audience can pick up your content and comment at their leisure. It's perhaps the most efficient way to find others with similar interests. You can then expand on those interests and never bother anyone who's not interested. There are no more Chamber of Commerce networking meetings for me: no more rubbery chicken, bad ties, and weird hair-dos. I can blog in my jammies or at the office, with the in-laws, or sitting in Starbucks."

Blood agrees that blogs connect folks made disparate only by distance.

"The main thing that surprised me," she says, "is how far it extended my social network. Blogging has brought me everything good in my life: my book contract, my husband, and my profession. I've traveled around the world because of it. When you blog, people can find you: people that are interested in the same things as you."

It isn't just professional bloggers and blogging CEOs that assert such things. Educators do too. Ben Rimes (www.techsavvyed.net), 26, is a sixth-grade teacher in Benton Harbor, Michigan.

"There are people out there," he says, "that you can tap into and that can tap into you. They're beyond your usual bubble. Within a couple of months of blogging, I established a really good friendship with a teacher in Virginia and another in California. We e-mail every week now and share ideas."

In posting his ideas for public perusal, Rimes wanted to surpass what he found on the Internet.

"There are lots of really great teacher sites that present technology and education as, 'Here's a really fun activity,' but I wanted to develop something that's a little more personal. I wanted to show teachers that the integration of technology can be more than a game at the end of a lesson. There are teachers just entering the profession that stare at the three computers at the back of the room and wonder, 'What do I do with these?' "

By blog-posting ways to integrate technology, Rimes did more than dispense. He received.

"There are teachers out there that have a wealth of experience compared to what I have. They might question my authority and wonder why I post what I post. But when someone responds and says, 'Hey, you can do it differently—and better,' that only helps my students out. I don't mind when people disagree with me. I actually enjoy it. It's better than having a bunch of people say, 'Good job,' 'Good job.' "

Thomas Woodward (www.incsub.org/wpmu/bionicteacher), 29, a technology trainer in Richmond, Virginia, also widens his world by blogging.

"It's a cool way," says Woodward, "for people to pool their power and help each other. You can construct a community out of people you've never seen. Not that many educators are geeks and some of the things I want to talk about are somewhat geeky. So, it's a way for me to talk to people that share my interests."

Like Rimes, Woodward enjoys the feedback.

"There are a lot of intelligent people out there. You don't know if your writing is good enough to publish. But on the whole, the community is really supportive and eager to help you out. That really cushions things."

Woodward sees additional value in blogging. "It's a nice way," he says, "to track your growth. It makes a record. To some extent, I use it like a journal."

Todd Seal (www.toddseal.com/rodin), 31, an English teacher in San Jose, has further uses for blogging. "It's a way to be transparent," he says. "It's a way to think out loud. I do the same thing inside of my classroom. As I make decisions, I'm always very sure to let my students know why. It also helps me sort through what happened during the day."

Seal also blogs for reasons beyond the classroom.

"I have aspirations," he says, "of being a writer. One way to do that is to sit down and write everyday. I have written for 31 consecutive days in my blog. I want to develop the discipline, the habit. And it's becoming a habit. I find myself saying, 'I can't go out and do that. I have to get my blogging done.' And blogging has developed in me a consciousness about writing. I now read as a writer and not a reader."

Believing that publication has altered his schema, Seal says, "My writing opened me to my scrutiny."

But for those that don't want public scrutiny, Seal suggests, "There are ways to blog semi-privately. You can password protect your blog so that only a few, selected people read it. You can use a pseudonym too."

Whether one's blog is fully public or semi-private, Blood says, "It's important for people to realize that when they're blogging, they are publishing. People can forget to set boundaries. When new bloggers are met with friendly voices, people can start to feel like they need to reveal everything. That's not true. There's a difference between personal and private things. Bloggers should remember that their words live on long after they've forgotten that they wrote them. Once something's published, it's fairly persistent."

If you still want to blog given the persistence of cyber-words, beginning is easy. "It's as easy as e-mailing," says Blood. And it's free at many sites, such as www.blogger.com. It's also easy to locate bloggers with your interests, via search vehicles such as www.blogsearch.google.com.

"It's worthwhile," says Woodward, "for anyone teaching to try out, at least for a couple of weeks. They'll see the power behind it: the power to connecting to a real audience and a real community. It's something special, when you get your first comment, when someone read something interesting enough that they took the time to respond."

Rimes agrees: "It's a chance to invite people into your world."

Although Shakespeare wasn't writing about blogs, for bloggers, this line seems apropos: "O, wonder! How many goodly creatures are there here! How beauteous mankind is! O brave new world that has such people in't!"

KATHRYN HELING
AND DEBORAH HEMBROOK

32

Publishing for the Magazine Market

Writing for the love of it is motivation enough for some people. But for most of us, the natural extension of that time spent at the keyboard is to share what we've written with others. Writing for publication is a gamble, an investment of time and effort that may or may not ultimately result in a published piece. For any writer, but perhaps especially for the educator-as-aspiring-author, magazines can provide a valuable springboard to getting that first byline.

If your dream is to publish a book, you may wonder why you would bother to pursue publication in a magazine. Here are some points to ponder:

- Your chances of ever being published at all are increased in the magazine **market.** Breaking into the publishing world is very, very difficult. Most writers try for years before having a submission accepted for publication, and some never achieve that goal.

Many magazines are published monthly, containing numerous stories and articles in each issue. Over the course of a year, this creates a high demand for quality writing, and magazine editors are constantly on the lookout for timely, well-written submissions. Simply put, you probably stand a better chance of being published in a magazine than in a book.

- Writing **for magazines helps you to hone your craft.** Most magazine stories and articles have specific word-count limits. Since beginning writers tend toward the verbose, the discipline of having to write within a word limit gives you valuable practice in being succinct and "tight" in your writing. If you're successful in selling to magazines, you will have learned to make every word count—a valuable lesson that you can apply to longer works.

- Magazines **may include features not found in books.** Short essays, poems, craft ideas, word puzzles and rebus stories are rarely published in book format. Yet these types of features abound in children's magazines and provide publishing opportunities for the beginning writer.

- Publication **in a magazine counts as a publishing credit—it gets you noticed.** Magazines pay very little (sometimes nothing) and you may have to give up all rights to your work upon publication. However, publication of any kind sets you apart from someone who has not had his or her work published. When you submit a manuscript to a publisher with a cover letter that includes publishing credits of any type, you increase your chances of getting your work into the hands of an editor.

- Publication **in a magazine indicates that your work stands out; that it was selected from a competitive field of other writers.** If your publishing history reflects several magazine credits, or a variety of features that have been published, you are demonstrating a scope and depth to your writing. It shows that you are determined and persistent, serious about your work.

- As an educator, **you are in the unique position of being an insider in your field.** You know firsthand what teachers need in terms of units, activities, strategies, topical articles and so on. Your teaching credentials give you status as an expert and the "edge" needed to get your specific piece published.

Once you are convinced of the benefits of writing for magazines, follow these tips for increasing your chances of publication:

1. **Do your homework.** Target the magazines that seem a match for your work and become *very* acquainted with the content, and layout of those publications.

2. **Look up submission guidelines on the magazines' websites or in resource books such as the** *Children's Writer's and Illustrator's Market.* Follow the submission guidelines for that publication to the letter! If the stated limit for a fiction piece is 800 words, demonstrate your professionalism by staying within that limit.

3. **Scan previous issues of your targeted magazine to be sure your story, poem, activity, etc., is appropriate for that publication.** Plan to read about a year's worth of back copies to get a feel for the types of submissions that might be appropriate. If your targeted magazine ran an article on fly fishing four months ago, the editors are unlikely to publish your article on the same topic, no matter how well written it might be. If you've read twelve back issues and not one of them contains a story featuring a talking animal, send your poem entitled "Jake the Giraffe Gets a Job" elsewhere.

4. **Don't overlook professional publications.** Teachers have ready access to a variety of professional publications, ranging from classroom tips and activities to articles dealing with current issues in your field. If you are currently working as an educator, you are in the enviable position of being able to try out your new social studies unit or art idea in your classroom-as-laboratory. Your conversations with colleagues and parents may be the launching pad for a research-based article or personal essay.

Whether you aspire to write for the educational market or the trade market, for books or for magazines, good writing deserves an appropriate venue. Many authors who make their living writing children's books got their start in the magazine market and continue to submit to these worthwhile publications. If you "make it" in the magazine market, you'll find yourself in very good company indeed.

LARRY LOEBELL

33

Writing a
Successful
Hollywood
Screenplay

Writing a successful screenplay that has any chance of finding its way to production in today's Hollywood requires that screenwriters embrace what is called "three-act structure." A three-act-structure script is heroic in design, with its main character accomplishing some seemingly impossible task after overcoming significant adversity. This structure underlies every genre from action/adventure to romance. While there are a small number of films that end in tragedy and still manage to succeed with audiences (and by tragedy here I mean that the main character does not succeed in accomplishing his or her goals), most Hollywood films follow a form that leads to the successful completion of a quest by the main character, even if that character does not survive the movie.

Three-act-structure films begin with a short initiating incident that propels the main character on his or her quest, usually a cataclysmic event—death (often murder) of a loved one, breakup of a relationship, or the discovery of imminent danger to the main character's community or world. The initiating incident shakes the main character out of his or her regular life and routines and forces him into new (and often uncharted) territory. The first act, usually about the first quarter of script, equivalent to one-quarter of the screen time of the finished film, typically includes false starts before the hero gets on the right road, as well as the introduction of the side-kick or partner who will accompany the main character on his or her journey, and evidence of the power and intention of the antagonist who seeks to prevent the successful completion of the quest. The first act is also where we begin to see what aspects of the main character's personality or personal history must be overcome for him to complete the quest. At the end of the first act, the main character is called upon to make the decision to continue. This might take a leap of faith, as the main character might be stepping off into the uncharted, dangerous, or unimaginable territory.

The second act is the bulk of the journey, usually comprising about half of the pages and the equivalent screen time in the finished film. It is marked by small steps of apparent success that are then undone by reversals of fortune and by obstacles. Some of the obstacles will be internal, fear, or doubts caused by the burdens of the main character's past experiences. Some obstacles will be external and completely unexpected. The antagonist or his minions may be responsible for them, or they may be mysterious, a clue to the puzzle that must be solved before the main character can move on. Some may be red herrings. These obstacles require increasing skill to overcome. The more obstacles there are, the greater the effort to overcome them, the more the completion of the quest satisfies the audience. Along the way, in act two, the main character learns which already-existing traits he or she can rely on to complete the journey, what new skills she or he needs to develop, and what characteristics are holding him or her back. The second act often ends with the main character having accomplished a great deal, but finally coming up against an obstacle that seems like it will defeat him or her utterly. This is the moment in romances when the newly confident lover discovers that the object of his or her affection is on a secret date with someone else. It is the moment in action films when the horrendous weapon of mass destruction becomes fully, horrifyingly operational.

The third act occurs after the main character has reached the low point, after the discovery, at the end of act two, that all of his or her good intentions and training seem about to fail. The main character must decide that there is no one else to accomplish the task at hand and rededicate himself to winning the day. This moment may be the result of an epiphany or the administration of good advice or a stern talking to, or the recognition of some essential clue. This turning point, at the beginning of the third act, propels the main character forward to completion of the mission or into the arms of his or her loved one. The third act, roughly equal in page and time length to the first, contains the events leading to climax and the climax itself. In this act, everything the main character has discovered along the way is finally put to use. The sidekick or friend is revealed to be important in specific, helpful ways. The antagonist brings the full force of his power against the main character, and the full spectrum of the main character's skills and inventiveness is brought to bear on the crisis at hand.

The use of this structure is so pervasive that an industry exists to help writers create screenplays in proper three-act form. Dozens of books explain the form in detail. Software programs that format pages and even prompt writers about what they need to include at every point are widely sold. Some even teach the world myths and literary conceits that constitute the theoretical underpinning of this structure. But understanding and mastering the technique is only one part of the requirement for success.

For a script to succeed, the writer must understand how three-act structure works for the audience, and create characters that deliver on underlying audience expectations. I would argue that we do not go to the movies because we want to be surprised by the outcome of a film story. Repeated viewings of Hollywood films written using this structure have taught us that the main character is very likely to survive the film, is likely to do something truly self-defining if not heroic, and is going to figure out how to best his nemeses and defeat his (and the world's) enemies, or win or win back the object of his love and affection. Audiences understand, because they understand three-act structure implicitly, that heroes overcome obstacles and prevail. But if audiences know that before they buy their tickets, then they must go the movies for another reason. It is this other reason that I think it is important for writers to understand if they are going to write successfully for this medium. We go to the movies because what three-act structure really promises is that someone with modest skills, even deficits in his or her personality or personal history, can overcome those deficits and use his or her skills to get the girl or boy of his or her dreams and/or save the world. Three-act structure suggests to the audience that whatever adversity a character might face, with the right training, carefully chosen allies or friends, and the right amount of gumption, he or she can beat the odds, overcome the past, put aside all former failure, and win the day. And that is a tremendously uplifting message. I would argue that that message, delivered by the structure of virtually every Hollywood movie more than by the story itself, is why we go to the movies, why we go back to films that follow this pattern time and time again, and why we re-watch our favorite films. Humphrey Bogart in *Casablanca*, a man with a dicey past, a drinking problem, a self-defeating antagonism to authority, a man quite like, well, every man, can be a hero to the world and the woman he loves—even if he loses her—by simply learning who his real friends are, outsmarting his antagonists, and pulling the trigger when it counts, even if it means losing his successful business and going into exile.

Individually and culturally we require this reifying message. We can become heroes if we just persist with an open mind or open heart, and a willingness to learn and improvise when the situation demands it. We appreciate the inventiveness of the screenwriter for creating exciting obstacles for our heroes and for creating antagonists who seem too tricky or powerful to overcome. We like adversaries that seem to possess limitless resources to stop our heroes from attaining their goals, and we love heroes who have complicated, even tragic pasts. But what we really crave is the underlying message: that anyone, no matter how humble his or her origins, Hobbit, Rwandan hotel operator, female iron range worker, orphaned son of murdered millionaires raised by their butler, in other words, potentially anyone sitting in the audience, can become a hero by persisting against the obstacles in his or her own life.

In my years of teaching screenwriting the most significant resistance I find to this structure is to the idea of giving the main characters flaws. But it is those very human characteristics that make us love our heroes. Likewise, villains who seem in all ways superior to the heroes they oppose are hard to write for some beginners. They resist the idea that the villain might be the more impressive character. But the argument that great heroes need great villains goes back to the roots of Western drama. Great villains give ordinary people the occasion to rise to greatness.

Reminding the audience that the requirements for heroism are human scale is the job of the screenwriter. Heroes and heroines who fulfill our need to see people with faults just like our own win the day are the reason we go to the movies, and any writer who forgets that is unlikely to sell a script in Hollywood.

SAMUEL TOTTEN

34

Writing Book Reviews Pays Off in Big Ways

Over the past two decades, I've written close to 200 book reviews for inclusion in educational journals (*Teachers College Record, Educational Studies, Social Education,* and *The Social Studies*), Holocaust journals (*Holocaust and Genocide Studies: An International Journal*), genocide journals (*Journal of Genocide Research*), and activist journals (*Fellowship of Reconciliation* and *Southern Exposure*). The payoff has been immense in a variety of ways.

Over the years, I've discovered that one of the best ways to keep abreast of the latest theories, research, innovations in the fields of education, Holocaust studies, and genocide studies (my three main areas of research) is to review books for journals. By committing to review a book, one not only has to actually read the book (ideally, cover to cover), but also respond in writing to what one has read. Reading the book, alone, is valuable in that one takes the time out of a harried schedule to plumb a topic/issue/idea in some depth. By writing the review, one generally engages in at least two of the higher levels of Bloom's Taxonomy: analysis and evaluation.

Reading a book and writing a review on a topic germane to one's field of research and teaching enable one to be more current and up-to-date in regard to what one teaches. Indeed, such "extracurricular" reading, at least in my case, has proved extremely valuable in the classroom as I draw on the new ideas/concepts and innovations I have read about. In turn, it allows me to be a good role model for my students vis-à-vis that goal of most, if not all, educators: being a lifelong learner.

No matter how many books one reviews each year, each new book constitutes an addition to one's professional library. Over the years, I have virtually built a professional library almost free of charge by requesting review copies of books (which publishers send out free of charge) and then reviewing them. Even reviewing only one book every four months means that one will have received four free books, the total of which is likely to come in at between $80 and $120. Who says it is difficult to earn "money" for one's writing?

Many educators, including assistant professors, I've discovered, are unsure as to how to get something published. Many seem to think that the "ins and outs" of the publishing world is a mystery. Well, it's not. And one of the easiest ways of beginning to learn about the world of publishing (including the process of "pitching ideas," submitting manuscripts, the author-editor relationship, copy-editing, etc.) is to start by publishing short book reviews. Once one grasps how easy it is to "deal" with editors and publishers, one's confidence rises; and when that happens, one is ready for a greater challenge—possibly, for example, writing an article for the same journal or magazine that has accepted your book reviews. The beauty of such a situation is that one already has a working relationship with the editor. Concomitantly, the editor is familiar with one's style of writing, the issues one is interested and/or has an expertise in, and that one knows how to meet deadlines.

Another valuable aspect of writing book reviews is that they are relatively short and the satisfaction one gets from writing one, as well as seeing it published, is capable of "stoking the fires" of desire to write even more—both more review as well as longer pieces for publication.

Yet another extremely positive result of publishing book reviews in different venues is that one's "name" is becoming noted by all sorts of individuals (others interested in the same issues as yourself, scholars, editors of books and journals, and publishers). More than once early in my career I had a noted scholar say, "Oh yes, I've read your many reviews, and . . . ." Name recognition is part of the "publishing game," and when one's name is "out there," one is likely to be asked to contribute to various writing projects. A case in point: as a result of a single book review I wrote on human rights, I was invited to write an essay for *Educational Leadership* on human rights education; the latter essay led to an opportunity to serve as the guest editor of a special issue (on human rights) of *Social Education,* and that special issue resulted in my being asked by a publisher to write a book on human rights. An anomaly? Maybe, maybe not. I like to think it wasn't.

As for writing a book review, a few tips are in order. Initially, at least, one should select books to review on those topics one has a passionate interest in and/or a certain amount of expertise. Those with a passionate interest in the subject matter will more likely write a review with "voice"; that is, writing that conveys a strong interest in the subject matter, an appreciation for the unique nuggets gleaned from the book, and an honest appraisal of the value of the book. Those who have an expertise in the subject can provide a constructively critical analysis of the strengths and weaknesses of the book, including whether the author offers any new perspectives and conclusions or not, whether the book includes any inaccuracies or gaps, and how the book compares and contrasts with the leading literature on the topic.

A reviewer also needs to "know" his/her audience. That is, one might review the same book in a radically different way for different audiences, for example, a review in *Social Education,* whose readership is primarily composed of social studies teachers, versus a review in the *Journal of Genocide Research,* whose readership is primarily scholars in the field of genocide studies. Writing for the former audience, one should avoid assuming a *deep knowledge* of arcane facts, historical events, and/or a body of theories and research—and yet, one should not speak down to the potential readers of the review. Conversely, when writing a review for inclusion in a scholarly journal, one can readily assume that most readers have at least a general understanding of complex issues on the topic, and thus the reviewer should provide a tough but fair critique of the author's analysis, use of supporting data, and whether the book adds anything of value to the field's knowledge base.

To be fair to the author of the book and to the reader of the review, one should read the entire book, and not just skim over it. As one reads, it is wise to make notes in the margins of the page or take notes in regard to key issues.

In fact, as I read a book I plan to review, I usually jot down key words, topics, events, personages that I wish to comment upon, and then each time I come across such, I simply list the page numbers underneath. That way, when I am ready to write the review I already know which issues I wish to address, and I also know where to locate insightful quotes and/or fascinating information that will provide the reader with a solid sense of the nature of the book under review.

Book reviews are generally easier and faster to write than an essay or book chapter, but how long it takes to write a review depends on the complexity of the book, the size of the book, and the length of the book review (scholarly journals often allow for reviews up to twelve double-spaced, typed pages, whereas teachers' journals generally prefer two to three double-spaced, typed pages). And, of course, if one chooses to write an essay review in which he/she reviews three or more books then that will take much longer to produce.

When all is said and done, writing book reviews is extremely rewarding. Concomitantly, one never knows who will read the review or what sort of offers will result of having someone read a review.

VON PITTMAN

35

Writing Columns for Professional Journals

In a long academic career, which has always included formal research and publication, I have found a means of communicating with my peers in an informal voice. In this sort of writing—unlike academic articles and research reports—my voice can be angry, provocative, strident, earnest, or even humorous (on a good day).

Opportunity

Ten years ago, the editor of the *Journal of Continuing Higher Education*, the premier refereed journal in my field of university-level continuing education, asked if I would serve as a contributing editor. My major duty would be to write a column of under 1000 words for each of three annual issues. The current contributing editor had written the column for many years and had decided it was time for a new voice. While my record of academic writing had been a factor in selecting me, and while the journal's articles were refereed academic works, my column should be informal, the editor said. I would be free, even encouraged, to take definite positions on current developments related to adult and continuing education. My positions could be supportive, skeptical, or critical.

I reminded the editor that I had a reputation for outspokenness on many professional issues. Some of my positions were controversial, to say the least. She said I would be free to change the column's focus. Fully aware that she was offering me a soapbox, she gave me only one specific charge: write a lively, even controversial, column in an accessible style.

My reputation for strong and pronounced views had attracted the notice of the board of directors of the journal's sponsoring organization. I had expressed my views in sessions at professional conferences, in my office's house organ, and in the newsletters of small professional groups. The fact that I usually had a definite point of view worked in my favor. For the first time since becoming a professor and an academic administrator, someone wanted me to be myself!

Voice

I began the column's transition with my first piece. To this point, the column had been limited to announcing or critiquing professional development opportunities, mainly workshops and conferences, in our field. Initially, I stuck to this theme, but focused on a specific area within our larger field, distance education. In my second piece, I announced that the column would thereafter center on distance education. My third offering announced a name change; the column would thereafter be "Distance Education Exchange." I told the journal's readers that it would consider any and all issues surrounding distance education; it would not be limited to professional development. It would, I warned, initiate—or better yet, extend— controversies in the field. As promised, the editor supported me in this transformation.

My first column after the change in focus was a strong advocacy piece on the value of distance education. The second had a more restrained and cautionary tone. Then, I presented the arguments of some of the field's critics, most important, university professors who considered distance education either a means of financially exploiting students and faculty or as a means of lowering academic standards. I asked readers to respond to pieces they didn't like, or even to those with which they agreed.

Burnout

At first, three columns a year, each ranging from 700 to 1000 words, looked easy, almost laughably so. But after about five years, I, like my predecessor, found that the ideas were beginning to come more slowly. The deadlines, as infrequent as they were, seemed more oppressive. It was time for a talk with the new editor, who had only recently accepted the position.

"What would you think about the occasional use of guest columnists?" I asked. "Instead of describing the work and views of distance education's critics, advocates, and innovative thinkers, we could seek them out and let them speak directly to our readers."

She saw the advantages of this approach, so I quickly began looking for guest columnists. Admittedly, the first few of them agreed to do columns because they were old friends doing, or returning, favors. One guest columnist drew several spirited responses, which columnists and editors always find gratifying. While I still write the majority of columns, the option of calling upon knowledgeable and/or colorful guests has greatly relieved the grinding pressure of the recurrent deadline. Guest essayists also introduce intellectual diversity to the column.

Breaking In

If you should be interested in writing essays in the literature of your profession, how can you get started? First, and not surprising, you must look for opportunities to build your credentials, your bona fides, as an essayist. This statement of the blatantly obvious may sound condescending, but I do not intend it that way. Building a file of published essays may not prove as difficult as it might initially appear. If you have published a scholarly article for a professional journal, write a short essay to describe, in general terms, your findings and their implications. Use it as a press release. If the institution you work for has a public affairs office, give it to them. They may be able to place it in the local press. If that is not possible, give it to your employer's house organ. The people who put out local newsletters are always starved for content, especially from a fresh source.

If you have not previously written for publication, start on a smaller scale. If you belong to some of the smaller professional organizations, or to the local chapter of a national organization, you probably receive newsletters from them. Volunteer to write essays or feature stories. Editors of small, or even large, newsletters often have to beg their friends (or threaten their enemies) in order to get pertinent content. The chances are good that you will get as many opportunities as you can handle. It is just as likely that the editor will ask you for ideas on feature stories or essays.

Advancing

Another means of gaining visibility as an essayist is to serve as the kind of guest columnist described earlier. With respect to the column I am responsible for, I always think three or four issues ahead. When I get a query about a guest column, I take it seriously. If an idea has merit, I want to find a way to use it. When the topic under consideration is particularly timely, I may even postpone for an issue or two one of the columns I have written. A guest column for a national publication, scholarly or otherwise, can create considerable visibility.

The downside of writing for small or local newsletters or guest columns is, of course, the lack of remuneration. However, there are upsides that may offset this. Only you can determine the value of the tradeoffs. First, you can build a documented history of publication that may serve as the first step toward more ambitious writing projects. And good writing is good writing. You can demonstrate and record your abilities as an essayist. Then there is the overworked term "networking." Your greater visibility, even if initially only incremental, should lead to further, and more prestigious, opportunities to get your work into print.

A Better Writer

Perhaps even more significant than the additional visibility you can gain as a published, although unpaid, essayist is improvement in your craft. I am firmly convinced that experience in writing short essays, with strict word-number limits, produces better writers. It is more difficult, page for page, to write a short piece than a long one. In a column, book review, or other short essay, a writer must choose words carefully. When given only 1000 words, or 700, or even fewer (I have been limited to as few as 400), each must count. Every paragraph must be carefully crafted. Thoughts must flow logically from one sentence to the next. The use of adjectives should be limited, while adverbs are best exorcised. You will become a better writer by producing columns and other short pieces, and almost certainly will become a more confident writer, prepared to take on larger, more complex projects.

Writing columns and other essays will give you a chance to take part in the dialog within your profession or discipline. Indeed, not only can you participate in the agenda, but also you should be able to help set it. You can have the pleasure of communicating in a non-pedantic, relatively informal style. From my experience, this can be fun, as well as satisfying.

SANDRA SUNQUIST STANTON

36

Writing for Newspapers

Busy educators don't always see beyond the enormous pile of things they need to do in the classroom, but reaching out to let the community know about school activities can have broad benefits. Children typically answer "Nothing" when parents ask what happened in school. What the children mean is "Nothing out of the ordinary." The community and the school both benefit when we share both the ordinary and extraordinary things that enrich children's lives and learning.

Community Contacts

When an educator is ready to share the rich experiences of the classroom, the media needs to be informed. Contacting small town newspapers is usually pretty straightforward. A telephone call is often enough to let them know about the program you're interested in promoting. The *Tri-County News* in Augusta, Wisconsin, published monthly stories and photos celebrating students chosen for supportive behavior. They were also happy to help us publicize our career development field trip to community businesses and thank the businesses for their support.

A week or two before a special event is scheduled within the Eau Claire Area School District (enrollment: 10,500), district staff writes a 500-word or shorter description of special events and sends it to Patti Iverson, Executive Assistant to the Superintendent. Without an official district public relations department, Patti has been trained by the Wisconsin School Public Relations Association to manage media contacts. She faxes the information to the local newspaper, *Eau Claire Leader-Telegram,* two local television stations, and three companies which manage ten radio stations in Eau Claire, Wisconsin. The system levels the playing field with equal opportunity for all media organizations. The *Eau Claire Leader-Telegram's* Education Editor is also helpful in answering any protocol questions educators might have. "Press Release Writing Tips" offers specific suggestions for writing news releases at: http://www.press-release-writing.com/10_essential_tips.htm.

Regardless of the complexity of the system, special projects receive the promotion they deserve, the school's public relations get a boost, and the media gets positive news. It's a win-win situation.

Writing, like every other venture, depends on networking. Staying in touch with local experts pays off in many ways. They know what's going on in the community, sparking pertinent issues for story ideas. Maintaining relationships and a current card file or Rolodex keeps contacts easy to reach for important local quotes. Inviting community members to visit the school also broadens awareness and support for school programming, paying off when referenda come before the voters.

Interviewing

Newspapers specialize in local flavor, so research involves beating the bushes for folks who have something to say about the topic. Finding and incorporating their information begins with staying in touch with local news. Once an individual is identified, interview skills become very important. The aspiring writer must:

- make the initial contact;
- schedule the interview;
- get signed releases for information discussed and any photos;
- be prepared and comfortable using technology to record the interview;
- communicate with the subject using Internet and telephone;
- transcribe recording into print;
- follow-up, double-checking facts for accuracy before submitting the piece.

Planning ahead and anticipating obstacles prevent problems. Some writers like to keep contact information, equipment, and supplies tucked into a bag ready to grab on their way out the door. Finding the interview location ahead of time eases last-minute panic. Trial and error can teach these skills, but it's much less painful to be prepared.

Step by Step

So, where does the story begin? After the topic is established, and the audience is defined, it's time for words on paper or whiteboard, depending on the writer's style.

Once all the information is gathered, formatting it into story format also takes careful planning. Story mapping was a technique I taught in classrooms, and it serves me well as a visually oriented writer. I have a dry erase whiteboard in my office on which I chart out each project in a story map. The title or topic is in the center in one color, with supporting topics in bubbles radiating outward in a different color.

I learned at conferences that grouping information into "magic threes" makes it easy to hold readers' attention. I cluster my supporting sections into three groups. For this newspaper-writing piece, the three sections are: Contacts, Step by Step, and Examples. In my story map, I used purple for the central title, Newspapers, and the three spokes dividing the sections. Using red for the details helps me stay focused. It also reminds me to write clear transitions as I cross the purple divider. A digital photo of the graphic is filed with my working drafts when everything is finished, making rewrites easier if I choose to pitch the idea to another publication in the future.

The Inverted Pyramid describes the progression of ideas as written for newspapers. We get seconds to convince someone sitting in front of the television to read what we've written in newspaper they're holding. The opening line must have a compelling "hook" that will lead them deeper into the story.

Start with the most important, and move into supporting details quickly. Editors look for a "Nut graph" early in the piece which summarizes the major points of the article. Reading that statement gives the reader a good chance to decide if they want to continue reading or move on to something else.

Sample Projects

Newspapers print objective feature articles or columns with a personal twist. Inspiring people and events show up regularly in schools. Letting others know about them builds awareness and support for the school.

For example, *Eau Claire Leader-Telegram* reporters wrote and published a story similar to those many educators could share. Bryce Johnson, a sixth-grade student, formed a Save the Rainforest club at Putnam Heights Elementary School in Eau Claire, Wisconsin. Club members researched the rate of rainforest destruction, and pledged to do everything in their power right here at home to protect the resources. The group also presented their research to the local school board. The school principal arranged to have a tree planted in Bryce's name at Yellowstone Park to recognize his accomplishments. The laminated newspaper photo of the group now hangs proudly on their In the News bulletin board.

Stories like these are all around us. Turning them into articles takes creativity and perseverance. Focus on a special project or profile an unsung hero. Collect the facts, add some photos or graphics, and let local media know about it. Whether they put the story together or invite the school's teachers or parents to write it, the community needs to know what's happening for students in schools.

Moving from "just-the-facts" feature articles into more personal column writing requires a different approach both in pitching it to the editor and in planning the column or series' sequence. Personal interest and expertise are welcome in this genre (see resource list).

One such series illustrates the nature of this type of writing. For the past five years, I've been a part of the B.R.A.I.N. (Brain Research Awareness

Integration Network) Team sharing practical tips for parents to support their children's healthy development. Everyone on the team is a volunteer (like me) or working while released for a short time from their day job. The team is a collaborative, independent group representing our two local hospitals, the area school district, Headstart, Family Resource Center, the Health Department and Department of Human Services, University of Wisconsin at Eau Claire, and community representatives. Sharing a vision with these individuals generates energy, enthusiasm, and lots of positive impact upon the community.

Connecting to community experts, I solicited and included quotes for the brain development series. A child psychiatrist offered suggestions to help parents deal with power struggles, a brain surgeon explained why bedtime stories are helpful to the brain, and infant massage techniques came from a maternity nurse.

The team opted to share recent brain research with parents in practical activities and small bits rather than long, involved summaries. We developed a cartoon character, Dr. Brain, which presents tips on each of eight basic needs for healthy brain development. The needs are:

1   Interaction
2   Good food
3   Touch
4   Language/reading
5   Play/exploration
6   Security
7   Music/movement
8   Rest/sleep.

Each need was the subject of a monthly column we wrote for the *Eau Claire Leader-Telegram* parenting section.

Face-to-face parent training is presented throughout Eau Claire County covering the same information. Newspaper publication of parent education opportunities increased participation, making the effort worthwhile.

Educators and newspaper staff help make each other's jobs easier when school stories make the headlines. With the right timing and communication system, everyone comes out ahead, especially the children we serve.

Resources

Associated Press Stylebook and Briefing on Media Law, Norm Goldstein, Basic Books, 2004.

The Elements of Style, Fourth Edition, William Strunk Jr. and E. B. White, Longman Publishers, 2000.

Flip Dictionary: For When You Know What You Want to Say but Can't Think of the Word, Barbara Ann Kipfer, Warner Books, 2000.

The Wealthy Writer: How to Earn a Six-Figure Income as a Freelance Writer (No Kidding), Michael Meanwell, Writer's Digest Books, 2004.

Write Faster, Write Better: Time-Saving Techniques for Writing Great Fiction and Nonfiction, David A. Fryxell, Writer's Digest Books, 2004.

Write on Target: A Five-Phase Program for Nonfiction Writers, Dennis E. Hensley and Holly G. Miller, The Writer, Inc., 1995.

Writers' Market: Where and How to Sell What You Write, Writers' Market (latest edition).

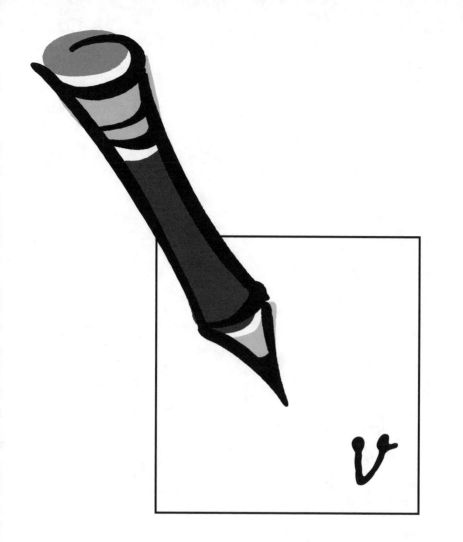

v

Book
Writing

CHARLES T. DORRIS

37

The Challenge of Collaboration

Several years ago, I worked with two academics that had researched how people visually perceive certain objects. The authors wanted to write a trade book describing their research as well as the implications of their findings on the design and interpretation of those objects.

One author was a senior person in this field of research, and her ideas were the basis for this book. The other author was to do all of the writing, which had just begun. The senior author wanted the book to be a best-seller, a book for a large audience, and a book focused more on the implications of the research than on the research itself. The junior author agreed with this.

Given the authors' agreement, I was surprised to find the manuscript containing more about the research than its implications, thus making it relatively technical and science oriented. The junior author finally admitted to me that he was really not "on board" with his coauthor's vision; he instead wanted a book for a more limited readership, a readership willing to "work" at understanding the research.

The senior author, who was also reading the manuscript, could see what was happening, but did not want to be drawn into the writing task, nor did she want to impose her vision for the book on her colleague.

These two people knew and respected each another and had written books for the academic world (although not with each another), and yet their lack of an agreed upon goal for the book jeopardized both their working relationship and the book itself.

This situation is virtually inevitable when the authors don't have clear and agreed upon goals for the book, for two primary reasons. First, the material in a book and how it is presented must be consistent with the book's purpose and readership. For example, the book being written by the academics in the above example would look very different if its primary purpose were to describe the research to scientists versus to describe the implications of the research to the general public. In every book project, questions periodically arise about whether to include a certain piece of text, an example, a graphic, or whether to explain a concept with more or less detail. These questions will often be decided by what is consistent with the book's purpose and readership—the book's main building blocks. In trying to resolve these questions, it will become obvious that if the authors are not using the same building blocks, they are not creating the same book.

This situation is also inevitable because it is so easy to fall into. Anyone who has written a book or memo or report (or what I am writing now) knows how easy it is to start without a clear purpose because we are so intent on telling our story, which of course will be interesting and relevant to everyone. Having a clear picture of the readers and how they will benefit from our story, this seems secondary. Some authors may even intentionally start writing without a clear purpose or reader in mind, because they plan to shape the material as they write.

This approach, however, can be a disaster in a collaboration given the difficulty of achieving a clear and agreed upon purpose for the book once writing has begun. And this difficulty grows exponentially as more is written because each author has more time, effort, and ego invested in the project. Also working against resolution may be the power relationships between or among the authors. In the example above, each academic had a source of power: the senior author had originated the ideas and had stature in the field; the junior author was writing the book, which his coauthor did not want to do, and he also benefited from the senior author choosing not to force her vision for the book on him. The result: a standoff.

In exploring how to avoid this situation, let me start with an analogy. Before becoming a developmental book editor, I was in the real estate investment field, and saw many partnerships, which are a common form of real estate ownership. The ones that failed were often those in which the partners did not have the same goals for the investment; for example, one partner would want to hold the investment for a much longer time than the other, virtually assuring a messy confrontation down the road. In contrast, the successful partners not only had the same goals, but they explicitly agreed on these goals from the very beginning of their discussion about becoming partners. In the same way, coauthors must agree on their goals for the book before the writing begins.

But the academics in my example had agreed, or thought they had. In academia, professional courtesy and collegiality are understandably important, but if they paper over real differences, they serve no one's interest. To put it somewhat differently, we have all been in relationships (professional or personal) in which it was easier to leave an issue vague than confront and resolve it when it arose. While vagueness may sometimes be the better part of valor, vagueness in a book project about issues as fundamental as purpose and readership creates a trap, a trap that will almost always be sprung as authors try to resolve the many questions that arise in the project. Coauthors must not only be clear but candid in discussing their goals for the book.

Is that all there is to it? No, not really. Even if authors have a clear and candid agreement about the book's goals at the beginning of the project, book projects evolve, and so do the authors' goals for the book. But if people begin a journey and unknowingly have different destinations, midcourse corrections become very complicated. For example, how do you decide that the new direction is better than the existing one if there is no agreement on what the existing direction is? Questions like this are further muddled by the controversy of, I thought we agreed the readers would be . . . , or you never said the book would be . . . To paraphrase a line from *Casablanca,* "This may be the end of a beautiful friendship."

There is no guarantee that authors in collaboration can avoid this outcome, but the odds improve if the authors have a clear and shared vision for the book at the beginning of the project.

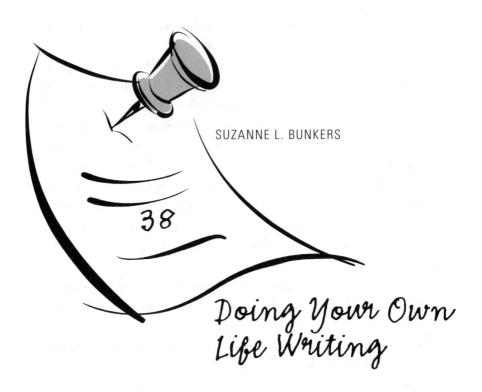

SUZANNE L. BUNKERS

38

Doing Your Own Life Writing

In recent years, more and more people have been doing autobiographic writing and enjoying it immensely. Some people say they are writing personal narrative, personal essays, or memoir. Others say they are writing autobiography, biography, or family history.

Whatever you call it, one thing is certain: this kind of life writing begins with the personal—memories of childhood games, holiday celebrations, first loves, turning points in one's life—and creates a story of the self within the context of family and community. Whenever I teach a course or workshop on techniques of writing personal narrative, memoir, autobiography, or family history, whether in a campus or community setting, I can count on having an enthusiastic group of writers, eager to remember and tell their stories.

Why has life writing become so popular? Perhaps it's because we're keenly aware of the passage of time; maybe it's because we'd like to leave behind a personal signature that says, "I was here." Perhaps it's because we share the human desire to create a record, not only for descendants but also for friends and relatives—a record that will survive in an age when diary keeping and letter writing are fast becoming lost arts as communication takes place via e-mail messages, faxes, and voicemail.

How can you benefit by doing your own life writing? First, you can gain insights into the times in which earlier generations of your family lived. Second, your stories can become part of the family record, helping to pave the way for future generations to know who you were and what their heritage might be. Third, life writing helps you gain a wider perspective on yourself, not only who you once were but also who you are now, and who you might become. Fourth, doing life writing can help you hone your research skills as you learn how to reconstruct the past and shape your story.

Like fiction, life writing utilizes strategies of composition that include narration, description, illustration, comparison and contrast, analysis, and evaluation. One additional ingredient in most forms of life writing is reflection, that is, commenting on how one remembers and how memories are shaped into stories. Yet autobiographic writing is not fiction. Life writing requires the interweaving of memory and imagination, the reconstruction and re-invention of the past, privacy versus telling of secrets, the role of dreams and memories in memoir writing, real time versus virtual time, fluidity of identity, self-consciousness in narrative, the role of lies and confessions, and the memoirist's ability to reflect on how the past has shaped the present and points toward the future.

Many life writers acknowledge and affirm the fluid (and at times contradictory) nature of "truth" and "facticity" (i.e., reliance on verifiable facts) when writing about their memories and experiences. Often, life writers shape their narratives in specific ways to help readers understand how memory and imagination can interact to reconstruct and re-create historical settings, events, and characters. Sometimes the reader even gets to "see" the narrator at work when a writer steps outside the text to comment on the significance of what he or she has just written. Such reflexivity sharpens the writer's focus and leads readers to ponder not only the writer's memories but also their own.

Like many individuals who do life writing, you might wrestle with the intertwined issues of integrity and "good faith," that is, honesty in your writing. You might wonder, how much can I tell? How much should I tell? How does the fact that my intended audience includes my mother, my siblings, friends, colleagues, students, and people I've never even met shape what I will and won't say as well as how I will or won't say it? These questions do not have easy answers. But they are certainly questions worth asking.

If you'd like to try life writing, here are several suggestions for getting started:

- Make a list of five questions that you would like someone else to ask if she or he were interviewing you. Then, write down your answers to these questions.

- Try to recall one of your earliest memories of something you did, a family celebration, a place you lived, an influential person. Make a list of specific sensory details (sights, smells, sounds, and tastes) and feelings associated with each of your memories.

- Remember the first time you realized that not everyone was alike. Jot down your memories of sensory details and feelings central to that time. Then, write about what you realized about difference as a result of that experience. Was difference in people something to be celebrated or feared? By whom and for what reasons?

- Think back to a time when you faced a turning point in your life, when you had to make a decision (or had a decision forced upon you) that would change the direction of your life. Write about how you made your decision (or how it was made for you). Then, consider how this turning point has helped to shape the person you have become.

- Make two lists: (1) "My Fears" and (2) "My Delights." Then, compare the two lists, reflecting on what you can learn about your values from each list.

- Imagine that you've written down many stories about your life and your family's history. Now, imagine it's one hundred years later, and someone has just discovered these stories in a dusty box up in the attic. Imagine who the person is who has stumbled upon your life writing. Write about this person and his or her reactions to finding your "buried treasure."

Now that you're ready to do some life writing, you might want to learn more about helpful books that deal with aspects of life writing and the role that memory and imagination play. For several years, I've recommended two favorite books on this subject.

First, I recommend Tristine Rainer's *Your Life as Story: Discovering the "New Autobiography" and Writing Memoir as Literature.* In her first chapter, entitled "The Story Only You Can Tell," Rainer writes: "The purpose of this book is to give you the tools to see story in your life, and then, if you choose, to give it shape in writing so it can be shared" (p. 2). Subsequent chapters in *Your Life as Story* focus on specific techniques for remembering one's experiences, then selecting specific details and using them to shape a narrative. A related online source is Rainer's website, "SoulfulLiving.com," which features online essays as well as writing prompts.

Judith Barrington's *Writing the Memoir: From Truth to Art* is the second book that I recommend highly. Barrington's chapters focus on theme selection, character, voice, tone, form, and narrative technique. Barrington defines one form of life writing, memoir, as "a kind of hybrid form with elements of both fiction and essay, in which the author's voice, musing conversationally on a true story, is all important" (chap. 1). On her website, JudithBarrington.com, the author highlights the importance of selecting details, highlighting themes, and developing characters. If you'd like to dip into this book, you can find the first chapter of *Writing the Memoir* online.

Perhaps you will discover, as I have, that life writing represents your attempt to come to terms with the tantalizing riddle of memory and truth in life writing. Most important, life writing represents an attempt to answer the question that each of us continues to explore: "Where did 'I' come from?"

Sources Cited

Barrington, Judith (2002). *Writing the Memoir: From Truth to Art,* Revised and Expanded 2nd edn. Portland, Or.: The Eighth Mountain Press.

Barrington, Judith (2006). "What Is Memoir?" JudithBarrington.com. 2005. 1 February2006. http://www.judithbarrington.com/writingthemem.html

Rainer, Tristine (1998). *Your Life as Story: Discovering the "New Autobiography" and Writing Memoir as Literature.* New York: J.P. Tarcher.

Rainer, Tristine (2006). SoulFulLiving.com. 2005. 1 February 2006. http://www.soulfulliving.com/discoveringjoy.htm

M. D. OSBORNE

39

How to Self-Publish and Still Keep Your Sense of Humor

So, you've written a book. And, for whatever reason (a colossal rejection file; a desire to do away with the middleman and harvest as many of the book's potential profits for yourself as possible; the need to create something from absolutely nothing), you're considering traveling the self-publishing route.

Are you really sure about this? Have you thought it over carefully? Because deciding to self-publish is a lot like deciding to have a child, and comes with nearly the same lifelong monetary commitment. And when those boxes of books are delivered to your doorstep, just like when you receive that squirming, blanket-covered bundle of joy in the hospital, there's no turning back. Both will even need their own room.

Still interested? Then let's push aside those nasty fears and doubts and get down to brass tacks.

The Basics of Self-Publishing

- What and how much you put into your book (time, editing, and money) is entirely up to you. The more aspects of self-publishing you can take care of yourself, such as the editing, illustration, or artwork, the book layout, the less you'll have to pay someone else for those services.

- Figure out how much of a financial commitment you're willing to make. Make sure you're giving yourself enough financial leeway to get the project done without breaking the bank.

- Keep the number of copies you print to a reasonable amount. You don't really save money by printing more books than you can reasonably sell (though printers everywhere will *tell* you that you will). The cost per book *is* less if you print a larger run of books, but unless you can think of something creative to do with the books you don't sell (like building a house with them or devising box-and-plank bookshelves throughout your entire home or office), you're in trouble. If you don't sell what you print, then you're stuck with cartons of moldering books that seem to stare accusingly at you.

- General rule for setting a price for your book: twice what it costs you to print it (forget paying yourself for the editing, printer cartridges, computer paper, design, layout, late-night cappuccinos or lattes, or any other pain-and-agony expenses incurred while giving birth to your book); otherwise, the book will be priced too highly to sell. Researching the market and looking at comparable books is a good way to help set your price.

- Realize that self-publishing your book will become all-consuming. You'll learn an enormous amount, and probably even enjoy the process, as long as you keep your perspective. And even though you become totally consumed by your book, keep in mind that many books have been written and published throughout history, and yours is just one more added to the heap! Back to the child analogy: a child born to you is precious, but, in reality, pretty boring to anyone else who has to listen to unending stories about it or who are forced to look at an accordion-style wallet full of adorable newborn photos.

Time for a pep talk. You can't extrapolate from any of this that because a self-published book doesn't sell, it means it's lousy or poorly written. I read books for a living and, believe me, I've discovered over the years that what's hot, isn't necessarily what's good. So, if you *do* decide to self-publish and don't sell out immediately, or even over the next year or two, don't necessarily take it as a sign that your book is a complete washout. The publishing and selling of books is a very competitive market. Just remember: Rome wasn't built in a day (and even while it *was* being built, a lot of slaves were enlisted for the leg work!), and, so, successfully marketing your self-published book will be an equally time-consuming process.

Get Ready to Get Busy

- Now that you've finished writing and illustrating your book, you'll need some sort of software to use for the layout of your book. I purchased Adobe InDesign and enjoyed working with it mightily. It took me a while to figure out how to maneuver my way through it, but it came with a helpful tutorial disk that I recommend everyone take the time to watch. Quark Xpress is another good piece of software. Both InDesign and Quark software are expensive (about $1000.00, respectively), but they are programs used most often by printers, and the ability to transfer your completed book into a format that printers can easily work with is a boon. If you're printing a text-only book, you'll probably be able to stick with a simple word-processing program such as Microsoft Word or WordPerfect.

- Design a catchy-looking cover. Come up with a blurb for the back of the book, one that captures the points of interest of your plot. If you've received reviews from a credible source, include those. What your Uncle Joe has to say about your book wouldn't be relevant, unless he happens to be Joseph Heller, that is. And don't forget to keep in mind the design of the book's spine. Imagine your book on a library shelf. How do you want the spine to look? Take some time with this part. It'll pay off in the end.

- Edit, edit, edit. Now's the time to call in all those relatives who have a knack for editing. Can't locate any qualified relatives?

Hire a college student to help with the editing. You'll hate yourself if you miss something during the editing process and see it rear its ugly head in the printed book. Trust me on this. I know. No one else sees those errors but me.

- Time to copyright your work. This is one of the easiest steps in the self-publishing process. The cost is $30.00. Check out the Library of Congress (LOC) website for a download of the application you need to include with a copy of your manuscript. Follow the instructions on the application. When your book is printed, you'll need to send the LOC a freshly printed copy to complete the copyright process.

- Purchase an ISBN (or *ten,* as is actually the case, for a cost of around $250.00 (in 2004). You can only purchase an ISBN number from R. R. Bowker, the official US Agency for assigning ISBNs. A book's ISBN is like a human being's social security number. It can't live without one. The R. R. Bowker website will walk you through everything you need to know, and then some, about ISBNs.

- You'll probably need a Library of Congress Control Number (LCCN). Spend some time looking at the first pages of any book you have handy. Pick one and use it as a guide to remind you what numbers and information you need and why. It will help you format the same pages for your own book.

- Keep your wallet open, because it's time to pick out a printer. Don't rush this part. So many of the websites for printers who specialize in bookbindery assume you know what they're talking about. I certainly didn't. I went with Signature Book Printing in Gaithersburg, Maryland, because the information on their website was clear and straightforward. When talking with a printer, don't pretend to know more than you do. Let them be the experts they are. Phil Nanzetta, the printer of my first book, couldn't have been more helpful. He was down-to-earth and all business. You'll need to furnish the printer with information concerning: (1) the type of binding (saddle stitch is the norm, but there are others); (2) the overall size of the book (which you probably already figured out during the layout phase when you used your snazzy, incredibly expensive software); (3) the weight of the paper you want for both the cover and the inside pages; (4) how many colors you'll need for the printing process (up to four) for the cover and inside pages; (5) if you want your book to be hard- or soft-covered; and (6) if you'd like to see it dressed in a book jacket (an addition of several hundred dollars or more).

- Submit your book's files to the printer, and empty your wallet. The final stage in self-publishing your book is probably the hardest: marketing it. This can be a distasteful chore to someone who enjoys the solitude of writing and/or illustrating books. But, with those newly delivered boxes of books looming like the Tower of Babel in your garage, basement, spare room, or living room, it's time to slough off the mild-mannered writer, turn on the charm, light up that megawatt smile, and sell, sell, sell. Let everyone in your family know that you're a full-fledged published author. (You'll be surprised at how many family members and friends *won't* buy a copy of your book!) Throw a party. Strong-arm your local librarian into buying a copy. Send out mass mailings to anyone you think might be interested in your masterpiece. Find a corner of the book market that is untapped and untried. My first self-published book (*The Boy Who Loved to Shim-Sham Shimmy*) is a children's story about a little boy who loves to tap dance for his grandfather. I sent out brochures to dance companies all over the country. I flooded public and school libraries here in Wisconsin with glossy, trifolded brochures. If your book is a children's book, offer to read it at libraries or schools. If it's a car repair book, offer it to local mechanics. Seek out your audience, instead of waiting for them to find you. List your book with Amazon.com or Barnes and Noble.com. Set up book signings at bookstores. Fortitude and grim determination here pay off. Have a friend, or yourself, if need be, contact the local newspaper and let it be known that your book has entered the building and is the next best thing to sliced bread. Keep good, complete records of your sales and expenses, right down to the last blank CD-R disk you bought to save your book's files on. If you treat self-publishing as a business, you may be able to write off many of the expenses of publishing your own book.

And while you're doing all this, start work on your next story or book. It's the only way to keep your sanity and your sense of humor. Self-publishing is work, work, work, no doubt about it. But ask me that one important question: *Knowing what you know now, would you self-publish a book again?*

Are you kidding? Absolutely.

RICHARD WEISSMAN

40

Textbook Authoring

Writing a textbook can prove to be quite a lucrative enterprise, depending on how common the course is, and the nature of competing books. Introductory classes in subjects like psychology or English composition have huge enrollments, and are taught on virtually every college campus. There are a number of interesting issues that surround the textbook marketplace that are somewhat different from the other aspects of book publication.

At research universities, scholarly and/or creative work are judged equally with teaching, when it comes to attaining tenure, becoming a full professor, or even receiving decent annual wage increases. At the opposite end of the scale are community colleges, where teaching is the paramount task, and where the academic workload can be two and even three times what is required at a research university. At non-research universities scholarly work is rewarded, but it is considered to be a task that is secondary to teaching. Textbooks are in a sort of gray area when it comes to scholarship.

Clearly, writing a textbook is preferable to not writing anything at all, but it is not considered to be a original scholarly work on the same level as a piece of "original" research. I place the word original in quotes, because the notion of what constitutes an original piece of research is not entirely clear to anyone.

Publishers of textbooks place a good amount of pressure on the writer for materials to be time sensitive. In other words, they want to see frequent revisions of a book, because otherwise students will trade in their textbooks, new students will buy the used books, and neither the publisher nor the writer derives any additional income from these sales. It is up to the publisher's sales personnel to hype the new edition to professors, and to explain that there's much new material in the book, that the professor needs to require that students purchase the new edition. Clearly, depending on the author, the text, and the subject matter, the actual need for revising the book is a matter that can create controversy, especially on the part of the students. Since textbooks are priced high and carry low discounts, most students, left to their own devices, are going to buy a used copy of the old edition of the book.

It is not difficult to make the initial contacts that enable a professor to leap into the textbook marketplace. All of the major publishers send book sales personnel to visit colleges, and they also often exhibit at national conferences in specific fields of study. Conversations with the sales people lead to them querying professors about possible new textbooks. Since these sales people visit so many colleges, if you float an idea for a textbook to them, they will often have some valuable feedback on your chances of interesting their publisher in your project. If they are at all interested in what you have discussed, they will then pass on to you an editorial contact with whom you can pursue your prospective text.

For teachers working at a kindergarten to high school level school, several strategies can be employed to access publishers. First of all, as a teacher in such a venue, there are already existing books that are in use at your school, some of which you yourself are using. It is always possible to contact the publisher with your own suggestion for a possible text. Just as college teachers are solicited by publishers to use new or revised texts, so will teachers, principals, and even school boards be contacted by publishers seeking to get schools to adopt their texts. The same general rules discussed previously apply: what does your text have to offer that isn't covered by existing books. Some of the factors involved are the use of more current research, involving a wider demographic population in your examples and history, and using a more interesting writing style, more current graphics, or including a CD-ROM, video, or CD when applicable.

It is not a bad idea to "test market" it on your own students, or the students of some colleagues. You should solicit feedback from students and other teachers. The great advantage of computer technology is it makes it easy to make changes in the book after this feedback. Be sure to exhibit the book at any state or regional teachers' conferences that you attend, and it is a good idea, should you get published, to make it known to your colleagues in your own school district, or even in your city and state. One way of doing this is to do a presentation on the book at one of the many in-service days that virtually all school districts utilize. From the standpoint of your school and the district that you are working in, it is a feather in their cap to have a textbook that comes out of their own program. These colleagues may well offer to share their own publishing contacts with you.

Addresses of publishers are available through *Writer's Market*. You should also look at educational journals, where the publishers who are apt to consider your work are likely to advertise.

To conclude, texts are a useful source of information for present and future students, and can provide an enjoyable and potentially lucrative opportunity for teachers. Professors at research universities, at least until they attain tenure, may want to concentrate their efforts on original research projects, rather than textbook authorship. For teachers at non-research universities and primary and secondary schools, in an era where administrators are moving toward merit increases in salary reviews, authorship is a tangible example of your stature and hard work in your chosen field.

CHARLES T. DORRIS

41

A Trade Book Is Not a Legal Brief

When I read a manuscript for a trade book authored by an academic, I often feel that I am reading a legal brief, because of how the material is organized. This style of presentation is not what most trade readers expect or want, thus making it more difficult for the author's message to reach readers, and even jeopardizing whether the book is read.

What style am I talking about? Non-fiction books typically involve an original idea that benefits a group of people, an idea for solving a problem in a new way or doing something differently or looking at something in a new light. This beneficial and original idea is the rationale for publishing and reading the book; in fact, the book's introduction may explicitly promise a benefit from reading the book. Many authors usually present the idea, its benefits, and how to use the idea, but also include the background about the idea, such as the research that underpins it, its theoretical or historical basis, how the author arrived at the idea, the problem that the idea solves, or the need that it meets. This is fine; it helps readers understand the idea and persuades them to use it. But it is in this background segment where academic writers fall into a trap of not adjusting their style to fit the trade book reader.

Too often the academic author explains the theory or research or problem, the journey to his or her conclusion, in great detail and at great length (in ways that I'll discuss below). It is as if a case were being argued before a jury of the author's peers. This style may be appropriate in a scholarly work, but it is not in a trade book.

While trade readers are as intellectually curious as the next person, they have a very practical perspective: just tell me your idea and how it can help me, and I'll decide if it makes sense to try it. They will be swayed primarily by the idea's usefulness and feasibility. This will be especially true of business readers who pride themselves on being practical.

Think of presenting the idea as a progression: the background, the description of the idea, how the idea benefits the reader, and how to use the idea to achieve those benefits. Most trade readers see the latter two or three segments as the book's "core"—the reason they bought the book, and where the bulk of the discussion should be. They see the background as an integral part of the story, but not the tail that wags the dog.

Before elaborating on this, let me introduce a related danger. The background discussion may not only be too long, but it may also not be related closely enough to the author's ideas. For example, in one book I worked on, the two authors explained their research using many lengthy citations from other authors; the background seemed like a survey of what other people thought, with the authors' ideas relegated to supporting roles in their story. This also occurred in another book where the authors presented a lengthy debate between two rival schools of thought—interesting to scholars but not to most trade readers. In the same book, a discussion about emotions and how many there are took on a life of its own, becoming an essay on a subject that should have been a supporting topic.

Imagine seeing a play that has a dominant character. This character is not on stage all of the time, but when he or she is not, the other characters are often speaking about the main character or reacting to what the character has done or may do. So the main character is always on stage in spirit if not in body, and the audience always knows that it's this character that is driving the play's action. In a book, readers must always see the author's ideas as the main character, with the background material as a supporting character. And this relationship must be clear in every chapter and in every section of every chapter.

To achieve this, readers must always be clear about why each piece of the background material is necessary. For example, one rationale for describing the journey to the author's conclusion is to establish the author's credibility. In one of my editing projects, the author spent several chapters discussing his twenty years of research in the fields of psychology, sociology, mythology, etc. This lengthy discussion was unnecessary because many trade readers would have granted him credibility, if he had simply described his credentials and briefly described how he arrived at his conclusion.

Closely related to this, the background should not tell readers what they likely already know. In another of my projects, the author proposed an alternative form of management to that of centralized control, and discussed in great detail the deficiencies of centralization as well as recent trends in management theory. This argument would have been insightful ten years earlier, but during that ten years, entire shelves of books had been written about it, and the readers of the new book, mainly businesspeople, would have been familiar with the argument. It was as if the author were using a checklist of topics that should be covered, building the case for the jury brick by brick. To repeat myself, focus on the edifice and what it does for readers, not on how it was constructed.

In addition to undermining the author's message, an excessive amount of background can jeopardize whether the book is even read. Usually background material is concentrated in a few chapters early in the book. At this point, many readers are not mentally committed to the book; they have not yet been "hooked." At this early stage, if readers feel the book is not what they expected (too theoretical and too technical) or they are having to work hard to get through the material, there is a real danger of readers putting the book down and never coming back to it, or jumping ahead to find an easier entry point, but in the process, skipping critical material. Neither of these outcomes is what the author wants.

Like a play, trade books cannot tolerate a weak first act. If at all possible then, put technical or theoretical material toward the back of the book. Readers are more likely to work through difficult material in Chapter 10 than in Chapter 2, because they will have more time and effort invested at that later point. Alternately, readers may not be equally interested to all of the background or need all of the background to understand the author's message. In this case, put the bulk of the background (or the most technical or theoretical parts) in an appendix, with a summary or the basics of it in the main text.

Sometimes, however, a lengthy background discussion is needed and logically needed at the beginning of the book. What then? First, consider creating shorter chapters technical or theoretical or research chapters may not be long in terms of pages, but they often "read long." Breaking up these chapters will give readers a breather. Along the same lines, use subheads to break up a chapter, use graphics to replace words, and use examples to illustrate theory. As a last resort, you can even put up a "road sign"; at the beginning of a technical or theoretical chapter (or in the book's introduction), tell readers that the chapter is atypical of the book. Admittedly, when I suggest these devices to my authors, some accuse me of holding the reader's hand too tightly. They may be right, but I'd rather err on that side, because when a book loses readers, the potential value of the book is diminished.

Excessive background reflects a style of presentation, and so, it may not be limited to the early part of a book. In any chapter, the author's main point may be preceded by background material that is too long and not closely related to the main point, thereby obscuring that main point, and undermining the author's message. Here again, the supporting material must clearly relate to the main point, and have a valid reason for being in the book.

In conclusion, trade readers have a different perspective from that of readers of scholarly works. Trade readers judge ideas less by looking back at how the ideas were derived, and more by looking forward at their perceived usefulness and feasibility. Trade readers see your ideas not as abstractions, but as concrete ways to improve their lives. They are more like consumers than a jury. Consequently, while the book should certainly include background material, this material must be presented in the proper balance, to acknowledge the different needs of the trade reader.

ANN RIEDLING

42

Writing and Publishing Trade Books

How to Begin Writing

How many of you have dreamed of having *your* novel or mystery displayed in the window of Barnes and Noble? I sure have! Once you have written, be it a journal article, a magazine column, a press release, whatever—it "gets into your blood!" Writing a trade book is entirely different from professional writing. However, "good writing rules" apply regardless of style. This chapter will discuss how to begin trade book writing, where to go for assistance and how to locate a publisher or agent.

Close your eyes and just imagine being a published author. Picture people coming to you with a copy of *your* book, requesting an autograph. Imagine how you would feel seeing this book displayed in a bookstore window. Think about traveling around the world marketing your brilliant new best seller!

A published book can provide you with more credibility than almost anything else you can do. Authors are highly valued in our society . . . and they should be. Writing a book does not have to be daunting or overwhelming if you follow specific guidelines, beginning with a strong plan and practicing patience and perseverance.

Below are helpful tips regarding writing a trade book:

1 *Genre:* Do you have your heart set on a mystery, romance, science fiction, cookbook, travel book? It is important that you know what genre you will be writing and who your target reader is.

2 *Title:* Discovering a terrific title is critical. A great title will not sell a bad book, but a poor title will hide a good book from potential buyers.

3 *Research:* No matter what the book is about, you need to know what you're talking about. If not, people just won't want to hear what you have to say. Then put you research materials into piles, one for each chapter.

4 *Outline:* It is vital to create an outline you can follow. This will serve as the blueprint for your book. You need to outline your purpose for writing the book, your theme, and stay focused on this purpose. For novels, develop and understand your characters and the roles they play in the book. Make them memorable, but realistic.

5 *Quota:* If you do not do this, you will become overwhelmed, and perhaps give up on your book. Give yourself a daily page quota to fulfill and then write that amount every day—no exceptions! I suggest three to five pages a day.

6 *Revision:* Nothing I ever write is the way I want it the first time around. Revising is an essential component of writing. Learn to edit, and do it well! Always go over you content numerous times.

7 *Feedback:* Obtaining quality feedback is very beneficial to improving your book. This feedback can be from a smart, trusted friend or relative, or a professional or editor. Listen and be open-minded.

Where to Go for Assistance

Fortunately, in this day and age, you have a wealth of information concerning writing, editing and so forth available via books, nonprint materials and websites. Many of these resources are certainly well worth your time and effort to read and/or view. Experts have created these resources to make your first, or second or tenth, writing endeavor much easier. Below I have listed some of the best sources for writing your trade book. Please understand that this list is far from exhaustive. Browse the web or your local bookstore to locate many, many other materials that may assist you in a wide variety of capacities.

Books and Nonprint Materials

Burroway, Janet & Weinberg, Susan (2003). *Writing Fiction: A Guide to Narrative Craft,* 6th edn. New York: Longman.

Bernays, Ann & Painter, Pamela (1990). *What If? Writing Exercises for Fiction Writers.* New York, NY: HarperCollins.

Cleaver, Jerry (2002). *Immediate Fiction: A Complete Writing Course.* New York, NY: Martin's Press.

Gotham Writers' Workshop (2003). *Writing Fiction: The Practical Guide from New York's Acclaimed Creative Writing School.* New York, NY: Bloomsbury.

Hahn, Pamela Rice (2005). *The Only Writing Book You'll Ever Need: A Complete Resource for Perfecting Any Type of Writing.* Avon, MA: Adams Media.

Novakovich, Josip (1998). *Writing Fiction Step by Step.* Cincinnati, OH: Story Press.

Script Perfection Enterprises (2005). *Power Writer (Novel and Fiction Writing Software).* CD format.

Websites

Storymind
http://storymind.com
Since 1997, this site has been providing articles, classes, tips and popular writing tools for fiction and nonfiction writers.

Write Any Book in 28 Days 1 Hour a Day
www.writequickly.com
This website, written by Nick Daws, is an online course for prospective book writers.

Learn Book Writing in NYC or Online
www.writingclasses.com

Gotham Writers' Workshop. NYC's creative writing school offers comprehensive classes regarding nonfiction, memoir, novels and more (offered online).

Where the Fiction Writers Go
www.fictionwriters.com
A website to figure fiction out.

Book Writing Tips to Live By
www.how-to-write-a-book.net/book-writing-tips.htms
Book writing tips can save you from falling into the crevice of writer's block.

Book Writing Software
www.Writersblocks.com

Visualize, organize, outline and write!
You are not alone. Use these wonderful resources to assist you in writing your book—the one you have been dreaming about for many, many years!

How to Locate a Publisher or Agent

A publisher might be a large company located in New York or Los Angeles, or it could be you, because the definition of a publisher is the person who puts up the money, the one who takes the risk. Remember, your right to publish is guaranteed to you by the First Amendment to the Constitution. You do not *have to* get a license or register with an agency. Bottom line: the publisher is the investor.

Overall, there are five ways to turn your manuscript into a book:

1   Sell your manuscript to a large publisher.
2   Sell your manuscript to a medium-sized (usually specialized) publisher.
3   Get an agent to find and negotiate with a publisher.
4   Pay a vanity press.
5   Publish the book yourself.

One thing you must understand about publishers—they do *not* promote books. Authors must do the promotion. Therefore, it is important to get a promotion budget in your contract with a publisher and let them know that you want to help make the book sell. It is also helpful to submit a promotion plan with figures to help the publisher wisely spend the money budgeted.

Medium-sized publishers tend to specialize in one or two niches, such as travel books and how-to books or poetry and memoirs. Therefore, it is critical that you locate a medium-sized publisher who is looking for the type of book you are writing. (You are more likely to be treated better by a medium-sized publisher—and sell more books!)

Literary agents provide three services:

1   They find a publisher by matching your manuscript to the publisher.
2   They negotiate the contract.
3   They may help you develop the manuscript.

The large and well-known publishing houses deal almost exclusively with agents, and many simply will not look at a proposal that is not submitted by an agent. You must realize that the average house is dealing with an overwhelming number of submissions. A survey of eighty top literary agents revealed they reject 98% of what they receive. The rejection rate for fiction is higher than for nonfiction.

Note: I realize you may be terribly discouraged at this point, *but* John Grisham and Tom Clancy both sold their first books without agents!

If you choose to use an agent, view various agent directories, such as the *Guide to Literary Agents* by Donya Dickerson and *Literary Marketplace* (newest edition). You can also get a list of agents from the Association of Authors' Representatives by logging on to www.publishersweekly.com/aar/

Vanity publishers produce approximately 6000 books each year. Usually, the author pays much more than the printing bill and receives 40% of the retail price of the books sold and 80% of the subsidiary rights, if sold. Many vanity publishers will charge you up to $30,000 to publish your book, depending on the length. (It's hard to understand why an author would pay that much when he or she could have the book printed for $1500 or less.) Personally, I am not in favor of this method of publishing.

Self-publishing isn't new. Many authors have decided to publish themselves after being turned down by regular publishers. However, many others have decided to go their own way from the beginning. Remember, writing a book is a creative act; selling it is a business. Some people can do both, while others are more creative than businesslike. You have to ask if you are capable of doing both writing and publishing.

Below are *merely a few* useful websites regarding publishing:

Expert Self-Publishing Services
www.arborbooks.com
This website assists you with writing your book and offers complete publishing services: printing, editing, marketing and design.

Publish with Xlibris
www.xlibris.com
The site includes a free publishing kit. Xlibris is a partner with Random House, Inc.

eBook Secrets Exposed
www.how-to-write-a-book.net/dt/t/ebooksec.php
This website discusses how to cash in on the profitable world of eBook publishing.

Manuscript Editing and Professional Services
www.book-editing.com
This site offers professional editing and other related literary services.

Ocean Cooperative: It's Your Write
www.oceancooperative.com
This website is a professional editing service.

Trafford: Fiction Publishing
www.trafford.com
This website offers self-publishing services for authors of fiction.

Free List of 400 Agents
www.AuthorsTeam.com/agents
This site provides a free list of agents to help you get published.

Allen A Knoll Publishers
www.knollpublishers.com
This site specializes in books mysteries, fiction, essays, children's titles, gardening and nonfiction.

Arcade Publishing
www.arcadepub.com
This publisher specializes in American and world literature.

Duration Press
www.durationpress.com
This publisher is dedicated to promoting international innovative writing.

Novel Novels
www.novelnovels.com
This website discusses the electronic eBook of novels.

Versus Press
www.versuspress.com
This is a small-press publisher for politically oriented writers.

Yes, *you* can be an author of that novel you have been dreaming about and talking about for years and years. Hopefully, you are now more equipped to tackle this project. It is *not* difficult if you create a plan and stick to it. Actually, it can be one of the most enlightening, exciting experiences you have ever undertaken. Write and enjoy! I'll see your picture in the bookstore . . .

DEBORAH HEMBROOK
AND KATHRYN HELING

43

Writing for the Youngest Reader

Do you teach young children in an elementary classroom? Are you a parent of an emergent reader? Do you have fond memories from when you were first learning how to read? If you answered yes to any or all of these questions, you may want to write for the youngest reader!

"Early Readers" refers to the leveled readers that many publishing companies offer for children who are learning how to read. The levels parallel the stages of literacy a child moves through to become an independent reader and writer. Typical headings for the literacy stages are: early emergent, upper emergent, early fluent and upper fluent.

Early Emergent Readers

Early emergent readers include patterns and are predictable. Patterned words and phrases help support a child that is just beginning to read. The child learns the pattern, looks at the pictures for clues and is able to read the words with little or no support. These early reading experiences help the child gain self-confidence which leads to independence. The beginning levels center around a predictable theme. For example, an early emergent story about getting dressed would have a different piece of clothing on each page. *My pants, My socks, My shoes, etc.* Many of the beginning levels are build-on books. This story would eventually end with the child dressed and ready to go out and play. It is important that the earliest leveled books have natural language and subjects that the child can relate to. Days of the week, months of the year and the four seasons are natural patterns that are included in many emergent readers.

Books that have a predictable pattern:

- *Brown Bear, Brown Bear, What Do You See?* by Bill Martin Jr.
- *I Went Walking* by Sue Williams

Books that have a building/cumulative pattern:

- *Today is Monday* by Eric Carle
- *The Birthday Cake* by Joy Cowley

Young readers enjoy "word play" in the emergent leveled books. Opposite words jazz up patterned, predictable stories. *Big monster, Little monster, Happy monster, Sad monster, etc.* Surprise endings keep the reading experience fun and fresh. *Nice monster, Big MEAN monster, EEEEEEEK!* Children love those sound effects!

Books that include opposite words:

- *Monkey See, Monkey Do* by Marc Gave
- *Dinosaur Roar!* by Paul and Henrietta Stickland
- *I Can Fly!* by Joy Cowley

Do you remember telling jokes and playing question and answer games when you were young? These word games can be incorporated into early emergent readers. *Is a shark a pet? No, not a shark! Is a crocodile a pet? No, not a crocodile! Is a hippo a pet? No, not a hippo!* At times, the pattern changes slightly, which challenges the reader. The patterned language is presented in the first half of the story so that the child gains self-confidence and independence. He/she has learned the vocabulary and is ready for a challenge. *Is a dog a pet? Yes! Is a cat a pet? Yes! Is a bird a pet? Yes!*

Changing the pattern makes the child pay attention to the print more closely and use reading strategies he/she has learned. As the emergent reader moves through the levels, the endings get trickier and trickier. *A dog, a cat and a bird. Yes! Yes! Yes! I say But Mom says, No, no, no!* The children learn about punctuation and other critical reading skills in a child-friendly format. Learning the mechanics of reading has never been so much fun!

Books with question and answer format:

- *Have You Seen My Cat?* by Eric Carle
- *What Would You Like?* by Joy Cowley

Young children can't get enough of those silly stories—the sillier the better! Books about stinky socks, gooey slime and naughty animals are just a few subjects that make popular early readers. Silly words and phrases just add to the fun! *Mr. and Mrs. Goober love garbage. They eat garbage. They play with garbage. They wear garbage.* Okay, we have the kids hooked into a silly pattern. At the end we break the pattern and surprise the reader. *HONK! HONK! Where are Mr. and Mrs. Goober? The garbage truck scooped them up!* Children will be laughing and enjoying every minute reading a book like this. Young readers enjoy books that are cumulative and have exaggerated or outrageous endings.

Books with silly elements:

- *Mrs. Wishy Washy* by Joy Cowley
- *Yuck Soup* by Joy Cowley
- *The Boogly* by David Drew

Upper Emergent Readers

As children move into upper emergent leveled readers, they are ready for rhyming words and phrases. Rhyming sets the stage for learning word families later on. *Mrs. Huggle liked to cuddle and snuggle. She cuddled and snuggled a rock. "Too hard!" said Mrs. Huggle. She cuddled and snuggled a flower. "Too soft!" said Mrs. Huggle. She cuddled and snuggled a teddy bear. "Just right!" said Mrs. Huggle.* Children can relate to this familiar pattern because of the treasured story of the three bears. Familiar words, repetition and rhyming words and phrases are perfect ingredients for an upper emergent reader.

Along with rhyming, rhythm is a critical element in an upper emergent reader. Some of these early readers are written to accompany a familiar song. Other stories have words that create a regular beat that can be tapped out.

One banana, two bananas, three bananas—peel! Four bananas, five bananas, six bananas—peel! Six bananas in a bunch. Six monkeys gather for lunch. Munch, munch, munch! eee-eee-ooo-ooo-ooo! These phrases have a definite rhythm and are fun to read and tap out.

Books that include rhythm and rhyme:

- *Mr. Grump* by Joy Cowley
- *Quiet in the Library* by Wendy Evans
- *Mary Wore Her Red Dress* adapted by Merle Peek

Fluent Readers: Early and Upper

Interesting and funny characters, setting and plot are components in fluent readers. Kids love reading about characters that get into trouble. They connect to characters that are having problems like being scared of the dark. And of course kids can relate to characters that can't figure something out no matter how hard they try. Fluent early readers have an escalating problem, a crisis and a solution.

Fluent readers (early and upper) with interesting characters and plot:

- *My Sloppy Tiger Goes to School* by Joy Cowley
- *Harry in Trouble* by Barbara Ann Porte
- *Alexander and the Terrible, Horrible, No Good, Very Bad Day* by Judith Viorst
- *Ira Sleeps Over* by Bernard Waber

As children become more fluent readers, they move into chapter books. The Henry and Mudge stories are early chapter books which generally have three "chapters" or stories. They have cartoon-style illustrations on every page along with the text. Junie B. Jones chapter books are for the more advanced readers. These books have more chapters and fewer illustrations.

Non-fiction Early Readers

Non-fiction early readers at all levels are in high demand. From dinosaurs to outer space to deep-sea creatures, this early reader genre is getting more and more attention. Even non-fiction readers can include patterns, rhythm, rhyme and other essential early reader attributes!

Non-fiction early readers (all levels):

- *Whose Forest Is It?* by Rozanne Lanczak Williams
- *In the Jungle* by Anne Miranda
- *Toad or Frog?* by Josie Stewart and Lynn Salem
- *Animals Change Their Clothes* by JoAnne Nelson
- *Way Down Deep* by Patricia Demuth

The best thing you can do if you are thinking about writing for the early reader market is to visit preschool, kindergarten, first- and second-grade classrooms. Observe children in work and play situations. Talk with them and listen, listen, listen. How do they talk? What words do they use? What books do they choose? Find out what the kids want to read over and over again.

Another great place to visit is the library and bookstores. Not only are kids reading in every nook and cranny, but the shelves are loaded with early readers from many different publishing houses. Talk to the librarian or bookseller, and find out which early readers are in high demand. Ask if there are any subjects or topics that are requested over and over again. This is excellent information to help you get to know the market.

Levels and guidelines vary from publisher to publisher. Most guidelines are available through the publishers' websites or upon request.

If you are interested in writing for this early reader genre, your goal should be to get to know the literacy stages a child moves through to become an independent reader.

What makes a reader? What gets him there? The silly words, the singing, the rhythm and rhyme, and of course a good story! Leveled books are skillfully written to take a child on a journey—to the moon and beyond!

KATIE MCKY

44

Writing the YA Novel

Ten Tools That'll Take You to "The End"

Want to write a young adult (YA) novel? Be warned: it might be the hardest form of writing. Based on acceptance rates, publication in magazines and in the nonfiction book sector is relatively easy. Only children's picture books have a higher rejection rate than YA novels. And YA novels can be compared to dancing with Fred Astaire.

Faith Whittlesey observed, "Ginger Rogers did everything Fred Astaire did, and she did it backwards and in high heels."

A YA novelist must do everything a writer of adult novels does, but with fewer and smaller words. And like Ginger Rodgers, you must step backwards, albeit in time.

Roald Dahl, the author of *James and the Giant Peach* and *Matilda,* said, "Every adult should drop to their knees once a day to remind themselves of how life looks from down there."

However, some adults don't need to kneel to see how the world looks through a child's eyes: such adults can't see the world any other way. Sure, developmentally delayed pseudo-grownups might be able to tie Windsor knots and prepare crème brûlée, but beneath their chin stubble and behind their haute cuisine, they remain children. If you have such a case of impaired development, it isn't all bad. If you want to write a YA novel, delayed development can be very, very good.

But to write a compelling story, you must be more than developmentally delayed. You must meet the adult challenge of getting your readers to care about your characters: by breathing distinct voices into them and composing compelling transformations. Then, you must cleave the fat from your text and pull the plot so taut that it hums like strung catgut when your readers pluck any page. How do you do this?

Gut-Hook Your Reader

Writing is a little like fishing. You must hook your reader and maintain tension, for a reader and a fish swim away if they're given slack. So, don't begin slowly. Begin in action. Or begin with humor. Your first sentence must compel the reader to read the second. Your first paragraph must compel the reader to read the second paragraph. And so on.

Let 'em Talk

Don't fatten your manuscript with superfluous description or a plodding plot. Let it clip-clop along. You can facilitate this by allowing your characters to talk. Writing dialog can be difficult at first, for it takes time for a writer to locate each character's distinct voice, but if you give them enough time to talk, they'll seemingly start chatting on their own. Rather than a creative writer, you'll feel more like a transcriber, following your characters around and recording their words.

Write in a Routine

Some say, "I write when my muse moves me."

Don't. Write in a routine. Larry McMurtry, the best-selling author of

Lonesome Dove, writes five pages a day, day after day. I write between 1000 and 1500 words a day. I am sometimes tempted to write more, but I've discovered that writing more for one day means writing less another. Don't fret about losing your flow. If you have a stellar idea, jot it down. Let it simmer in your subconscious. It'll still be there, nice and ripe, when you rise to write the next day. And rising to write, day after day, produces a novel. Sixty 1000-word days is the typical 60,000-word YA manuscript.

Millions of novels are begun. Few are finished. So, train your imagination to be a steady tap from which a measured amount of words flows.

Be a Butcher

When you write everyday, you produce, over time, a hefty word count. This allows you to be a butcher. Wield the delete key like a cleaver, whacking off fat.

One way to determine if your manuscript is lean is to write a single sentence that delineates the purpose of each chapter. Each chapter should have a unique purpose. For example, if you have three chapters that show that your hero is a daring kid, cut two of those chapters.

Writing isn't parenthood. Parents aspire to love all their children equally. Don't do so with your prose. Be harsh. Save the best. Toss the rest.

When you're harsh, you love your story more than you love yourself. If your intent is to show everyone how clever you are, to shift your readers' attention from you to the story with lyrical language, perhaps poetry is a more apt format for you. If you write a lean enough story, it will do more than clip-clop: it will gallop. And a galloping story is one that YA readers will ride.

Respect Your Reader

Be especially harsh when it comes to preachy and teachy prose. Save preaching for the pulpit and teaching for the classroom. Your job, as a storyteller, is to tell a story.

Dr. Spock began his best-selling book with, "You know more than you think you do."

Likewise, your YA readership will know more than you think they know.

So, don't make commentary part of your YA novel. They can comment on their own.

Childhood Is Gothic

Yes, childhood is shadowy. Must adults have forgotten how dark it is beneath a child's bed. Monsters bunker there. And bad men lurk in bushes. Everything is more intense, for the tongue tastes more and the ears hear more. Young soles and souls do not yet have calluses between them and the world. The world is more vivid, grander, and more terrible. So, the children's stories that endure are Gothic. Beautiful girls are fed poisoned apples and entombed alive in glass coffins. Awful aunties torture a sweet boy, who then flees with a spider and other creepy-crawlies, only to be preyed upon by steel sharks and phantom pirates. Poor little girls are sent out on Christmas Eves, to sell matchsticks, freeze, and die. Boys are incarcerated in a desert and forced to dig holes. Whereas most children do not face such perils in their waking lives, they do in their imaginations, so they will relate to the dank, foggy sensibilities of a Gothic tale.

Let It Get Bad

To tell a Gothic tale, you have to let it get bad. Deeply, darkly bad. Now, letting it get bad is good because it can't get better in a story unless it first gets bad. Letting it get bad also gives your characters a chance to test their mettle. Conflict, deprivation, and loss are the flames that will temper your characters and make metal of their backbones.

Let Them Fail

Letting your characters fail will help your readers believe that they are real. It also helps them to care about your characters.

Anne Morrow Lindbergh wrote, "In the final analysis, we are all alone."

And she's right. We are all alone and more than that, we are all self-absorbed. Although we are each a world of one, there are some congruencies. For example, every person knows shame. Everyone knows how it feels to be insufficient. All of us have been giddy. We've all known folly.

Allow faults to marble through the characters of your characters. Then, they won't just be more engaging. Your readers will be able to relate.

Live Like a Thief

Writers don't conjure characters out of the mist of their imaginations. Writers, as Picasso once said of painters, "Steal, steal, steal."

So, live like a thief. Talk less. Watch more. Just as a thief cases out a bank before the big heist, you too need to case out life before writing about it.

Note what people, both big and small, say and do. Some of the most prolific writers, like Garrison Keillor and Stephen King, are introverts. Introverts don't fritter their days away with jibber-jabber. They listen. They watch. Do the same. If this sounds like a solitary life, it is. The schmoozing comes later, when you're promoting your first YA novel.

Getting to the End

Beginning a YA novel is easy. The hardest and greatest two words you'll ever write are "The End." To be a writer, you must write. You must find a way to keep your seat on the seat of the chair.

Squeeze yourself into routine. Write in the same place at the same time, day after day.

You can deprive yourself of what you love, until you write the requisite words. For example, I love to walk through the park that is adjacent to my house, but I dangle that park before me like a carrot. I don't get to walk until I write.

Write is a verb. If you don't write, you aren't a writer. You're a wisher. I can understand why folks would rather wish than write. Writing is hard work. Wishing is easy. Wishing is akin to gazing across the dance floor at a cute guy, smiling, and then leaving.

Writing is working up the nerve to talk to him and then working up the gumption to commit to him. Writing, like love, is a leap of faith, for few beginning writers ever began a book with promises or contracts, but to create characters, you must test your character. Your resilience. Your faith.

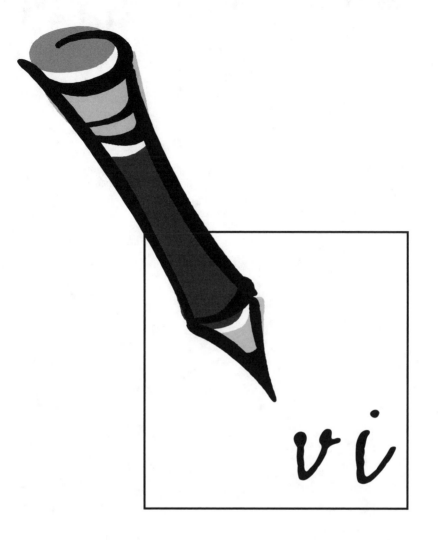

vi

Writing
Life of a
professional

GLORIA NIXON-JOHN

45

Avoid the Ego-Driven Process Like Quicksand

I grew up watching Sunday afternoon jungle movies, and in those movies someone (usually wearing loin cloth and saber-tooth necklace) inevitably ended up struggling in quicksand. Few survived the terra firma turned mush unless there just happened to be someone with long arms and a long stick nearby. The good guy usually did have such a person around, the bad guy . . . a goner . . . three bubbles and goodbye. I suffered terrible quicksand nightmares as a child, but I am glad to say that they have stopped and haven't been replaced by the high-tech horrors available on television and in movies today. Still, I am hard-pressed to find a life-threatening quandary as disturbing as the thought of sinking into quicksand. Lucky for me there is no physical threat of this happening anytime soon. When I find myself "sinking" these days, it is usually related to some fear of personal loss or failure. And, admittedly, I had that sinking feeling more often than not when I first started to take my writing seriously. This happened because once I began to take myself seriously I knew that serious criticism was not far behind. So, I guarded myself again the trauma of criticism, constructive or otherwise, by seeking out readers who were not writers, many were not avid readers either. I asked friends, relatives, even strangers, to read my poems, essays, and stories, and avoided going to anyone I thought might know more than I did about writing. I thought it shrewd of me to give my writing only to those non-writers who would marvel at the ingenuity of a particular metaphor, or the carefully selected verb, simply because they were seldom called to write in such a way themselves, or didn't know that there was a lot of writing out there equally as clever, and much better. I knew, going in, that these well-intending souls would think me clever. But, of course, this strategy wasn't shrewd at all. It was more or less just a gesture intended to elicit praise. It was something I did for the sake of my fragile ego, not for the good of my art. The egotist in me wanted to avoid the quicksand of criticism. I like what Barbara Stanwyck once said about "Egotism . . . (that it is) usually a case of mistaken nonentity." Frank Leahy puts it this way: "Egotism is the anesthetic that dulls the pain of stupidity." Both quotes lend themselves well to what I was doing by avoiding constructive criticism of my writing. And, it has taken me a good twenty years to get over myself enough to happily revise a piece of writing upon the advice of good authority. Let me explain what happened over the course of those twenty years. Don't worry; I will give you the condensed version. Of course, I am sorry that this realization took me a long twenty years. Perhaps, I can help make the journey a little faster. Journey? Where, do you ask? The journey that gets you to the point where you are writing for the sake of the writing, intent on publishing perhaps, but willing to do what it takes to make the writing the best that it can be. No short cuts, no avoidance behavior whipped up by your fragile ego.

The first thing that had to happen, and did in my case, was that I began to think of myself as a writer. Not a teacher who sometimes writes. A writer. With my new identity in mind, I joined writers groups composed of people who wanted to be writers (not teachers who write but think of themselves as teachers first . . . I know I am stepping on toes here, but this is important so bear with me). I had tried the writers groups that are composed mostly of teachers who tinker with writing, and those groups usually turned out to be mostly about teaching writing, not about doing any serious writing. I think my fragile ego led me to these groups. No, I know it did. They were, for the most part, local and state writing groups that had their sights on something other than developing and supporting each other as writers. Some were mostly social groups, others were teacher groups. But what these writing venues, projects, clubs, had in common was that they were infected by an acceptance of mediocrity. Most knew what they were doing was self-congratulatory and patronizing, but also believed that those writing (especially in the case of English teachers) were to be congratulated for writing at all, and should therefore be treated gently. My ego loved it because in many of these groups I was the more experienced writer and little was said that was critical. It was safe. No quicksand. But it felt wrong, felt like a waste of time. And, I even began to believe that a sinking feeling was better than no feeling at all. With my husband's urging I got brave and went off to writing workshops that were filled with working writers from all walks of life, and led by practicing writers. At first I felt like I had placed myself at the lip of not just a quicksand pit, but at the lip of a steamy-mouthed volcano where my writing was going to be scrutinized by professional writers (some of whom were teachers, but that was beside the point). I was inspired by the likes of Leon Uris, Stephen Dunn, Dutch Leonard, Joy Williams, and Anne Beattie to name a few. And, believe me when I say there was no patronizing allowed. The constructive criticism came in bushels full, and it was always on point, sometimes painful. But, it was what was going around. Everyone was getting it. These workshops (invitations to which can be easily found in *Poets and Writers Magazine*) were replete with models of good writing, and held together by a community that was there to write and improve their writing, led by people who give their lifeblood to the craft. I could not have survived these legitimate, focused writing workshops if I had gone there for praise.

The second thing I did was to read more and to read with an eye and ear for style and craft. This was so carefully demonstrated in the worthwhile workshops I attended that it was just a matter of continuing. While I had spent much of my life dissecting literature in order to write the literary criticism necessary in undergraduate and graduate programs, I learned instead to keep a little question in my head as I read. The question being, am I writing as well as this writer? When I asked this question of myself, the answer came down to a comparison of style and craft, and whether or not I had an identifiable, different, and compelling voice. Putting this another way, I became my own critic and I measured myself against the best possible writing I could find. In many cases, sad to say, I had to say, no I am not as good as this writer or that. But, as time passed I was saying yes more often. Soon I realized that what separated me from those who surpassed me was sometimes simply the time and effort they were putting forth that I was not. But I also had to admit that I could never measure up to some. That was ok too. That gave me writers to worship, not a bad thing for a writer to do.

The third thing I did to move away from my previous ego-driven process was to ignore all of the books I had bought over the years about teaching writing, teaching revision, teaching, teaching, and teaching. I went straight to books by published writers who had written about the art and craft of writing. I read Stephen King's *On Writing*. Marvelous! How mainstream you are thinking. Nonsense. Get over yourself, as Stephen might put it. This little gem of his is well written, on point, and entertaining. Imagine that. I also depend on Mary Oliver's *A Poetry Handbook*. She teaches with good models, doesn't patronize while dealing with the craft, substance, and spiritual underpinnings of good poetry. I like Annie Dillard's *The Writing Life* too. It calms me down. Gets me to focus. She allows me to, no she insists that I, move the ego aside so that I can find the subject and space wherein I can tap into what I really know, which is usually also what I really want to write about. The permission that Annie Dillard gives me led me to write a memoir about growing up on Detroit's East Side. No money changed hands when I did this writing, no one said "Marvelous;" the writing came from a place that is memory, reflection, heartache, joy, and a million questions. There is no place for ego when I am there and my motivation is intrinsic. Of course, there are many good books written by real writers. I have shared these three because they are at my fingertips and are dog-eared.

In brief summary, if you are serious about your writing, don't waste your time in writing groups that do nothing more than inflate your ego. Go to the experts who walk the walk, and hear what they have to say. The constructive criticism you get there will buoy you up later, I promise. Next, read, not about teaching writing, but read what writers have to say about style, craft, substance, and voice. And when you read good poems, essays, and fiction, read as a writer does. Ask yourself how your writing measures up. Only then will you be on terra firma, free of the way the ego might drag you down.

GLORIA NIXON-JOHN

46

Back to the Future with Qualitative Research

There are so many times in my life when I am thankful that I crossed paths with a particular teacher. Diane Brunner (once at Michigan State University) is one of those teachers. Of course, I didn't realize how I would use the instruction and insight she gave so graciously. I didn't realize, couldn't imagine, how the qualitative research methods she taught me would fit into the "ice nine" age of information technology. In fact, I was taking a university required computer class (disguised as a course in rhetoric) at the same time I was taking Diane's class called the Ethnography and Design of Qualitative Research. The two courses seemed at odds. I realize now that both were necessary. But, in my writing life, the qualitative research course has proven the most valuable of the two. As part of Dr. Brunner's course, students were asked to use any one of a variety of interview methods in order to gather raw, first hand information that we were then expected to scrutinize carefully in order to reach some conclusions about our chosen subject. The conclusions would, quite naturally then, become a part of a paper. I decided to use the Seidman method to interview my chosen subject, a twentieth-century teacher who was teaching in a nineteenth-century one-room school house. The information and insights I gleaned from the qualitative approach to this research were stunning to me. And, I know that the traditional forms of research, or research in a library or on the web, would not have gotten me anywhere near to what I learned going about this in the direct and someway pure approach inherent in the qualitative method. And, now, whenever I approach a research project using just libraries and the web I feel a bit cheated, feel like I am doing something less authentic than I could be doing. Feel like I am not learning all there is to learn. The conclusions I reached about the one-room school house teacher are the subject for another, longer article. But, in a nutshell, I learned how her life, as both a child, then as an adult, led her to her teaching position at that school. I also learned that what she was doing was as much progressive as it was old. For purposes of this chapter, however, I want to share the Seidman method with you and tell you why it is a valuable tool. I then want to share where it has led me in terms of how I write and what I am writing now.

Dr. Seidman will have to forgive me for giving you my somewhat skewed use of his method. But, I will indeed reference his book at the end of this article so that you can check it out for yourself. Basically, this method suggests that you meet with the subject of your research for a series of interviews. I decided on three interviews of one hour each. In the first interview, I asked the subject to tell me about her life as a child, or her life growing up, to put that life in its original context and to say anything she wanted to about it. I had the tape recorder on and my role was to, more or less, just nod or ask short questions when she seemed to need a nudge. She did 95% of the talking. What she told me in that first interview was informative, detailed, and rich. I learned about her difficult childhood, her insinuated (by circumstances) nurturing approach with regard to others. At our second meeting some two weeks later I asked her to tell me about her life in the present. Again, her response came rolling out with ease (with a few tears as well). I tried not to cry along with her, had tissue ready as I learned about her work life and her personal life. She was (no surprise here) about to adopt a child. And, she made clear that her students were a part of her community in every sense of the word *community*. Interaction among teacher, parents, and child was a given. The third question, Tell me about how your years growing up (or the things you told me in that first interview), are connected to what you do now, how your life is now. At times I had to remind her what she said in those first two interviews. I had the transcripts available at this third interview so that I wouldn't be tempted to translate what she had to say in my own words. The connections she made astounded me and left me in awe of her life, her choices, and her vocation. I learned that having had several siblings to care for, work on a Michigan farm surrounded by her eight younger siblings, led her toward a teaching situation in which she could work with the students in a reciprocal, giving way, one in which peers were expected to help peers. (No, we did not invent peer tutorials in 1975.) I also learned that her role was quite naturally more than that of instructor. Lawyers across America will cringe when I say that this teacher even took to washing her students' hair if it needed washing. If someone came in late and cold because they had missed the bus, she asked one of her older students to go into her classroom kitchen to brew up a kettle of hot cocoa. She kept a supply of dry socks in various sizes handy too. Did her students learn? Academically they learned as well as those in the public and private schools in the area. They even mapped out what they were learning (had failed to learn) and what else they hoped to learn all evident on a big chart they put up on the wall (curriculum mapping). And, what they learned about caring and community, even sportsmanship, was not just for those who made it onto a playing field. It was the reality of life lived in the one-room school house. To tell you that what I discovered from this research was surprising is an understatement. I was astounded and in awe of what I learned.

Needless to say I have since used this approach with my students because I believe that the qualitative method is not just worthwhile but has become more necessary insomuch as our students are going to the Internet thinking that all the information they will ever need is there and that what is found there can be trusted. On the teacher end, the qualitative method will make it easier for you to read those research projects lest you get thirty papers with the same six sources and the same conclusions. You, and they, will learn from, and bask in, real primary information, not the primary information found in the library or on the Internet—twice removed.

I promised that I would tell you where this method has led me. Clearly it has led to a change in the way in which I teach and approach research. But, it has also opened me up to opportunities as a writer. In the writing community, the one outside of education, I have been called upon to generate a variety of texts using this method. The latest of which is a novel based on a true story about the youngest American to have served on death row. Much of the information for this novel is based on interviews that I have and continue to conduct with the psychologist involved in this case, as well as the attorneys, even prison cell mates, of the accused. In several of the interviews I have used the Seidman method. In other interviews I had to use other interviewing techniques. But, I could not do this writing without using this primary, qualitative, approach. The intellectual discussions you can find about this approach do not come with warnings about the importance of appropriate procedure, about the ethics and necessity to tread lightly around various subjects and topics. So, I suggest you do some reading before you head out with tape recorder and note pad. But, do head out with tape recorder and note pad eventually. And, send your students out armed with this method as well. The twenty-first century demands that you do.

Suggested Sources

Bell, Susan Groag & Marilyn Yalom (1990). *Revealing Lives: Autobiography, Biography, and Gender.* Albany: State University of New York Press.

Seidman, I. E. (1991). *Interviewing as Qualitative Research: A Guide for Researchers in Education and the Social Sciences.* New York: Teachers College Press.

Silverman, David (2005). *Doing Qualitative Research: A Practical Handbook.* London: Sage Publications Inc.

Wengraf, Tom (2004). *Qualitative Research Interviewing: Semi-structured, Biographical and Narrative Methods.* London: Sage Publications Inc.

M. D. OSBORNE

47

*Blueprints
for Building
a Writer's Website*

What's more exciting than actually writing and finishing a book? Why, getting it published, of course. It's quite an achievement. So, go ahead and bask in the glow of your accomplishment—but don't get too cozy. There's still work to be done. Whether the book you've written is published by an established publishing house, a small press, or if you've decided to self-publish (*especially* if you've decided to go this route), you'll still need to take a hand in your own promotion. And an essential step in that promotion is building and maintaining an author's website. A writer's website probably won't provide you with a lot of additional book sales (only about 10% of book buying actually occurs on the web), but it *is* a place for you to refer people who want to learn more about you and your writing. The number of people who have access to a writer's website is staggering, but whether or not they manage to find you in the vast, Internet thicket is an entirely different matter.

You can think of a writer's website as a twenty-four-hour-a-day business card. And in the same way that you may decide to hire a professional to design and print your business cards for you using the information you provide, you can hire someone to build and design your website. Bear in mind, however, that web design can be costly. However, you may decide to take the creative plunge and use one of the do-it-yourself website building tools available today (software, sites on the Internet that hold your hand and virtually walk you through the website building process for a reasonable fee, etc.). It's up to you. Designing your own website can actually be quite a bit of fun. I've known many people who claimed to have very little computer savvy come up with quite passable websites using Front Page or Adobe's GoLive programs. I chose to build my website using the same company, Register.com, from whom I purchased my domain name. (The Domain Name System [DNS] helps users to find their way around the Internet. Every computer on the Internet has a unique address—just like a telephone number for a telephone. For instance, my domain names are www.woodenshoepress.com and www.mdosborne.com. You purchase the use of a particular domain name for a specified amount of time—usually one, two, or three years. The costs seem to vary, depending on where you look on the Internet, so shop around until you feel satisfied that you're getting the best deal.) An Internet search for domain names, and/or building your own website, will furnish you with more information on where to begin than you may be able to comfortably digest in one sitting. The design of your website is ultimately up to you. Can you live with the somewhat generic templates available at create-it-yourself site builders on the web, or would you prefer a highly customized, sophisticated design for your site? More developed and sophisticated will probably mean, of course, a higher cost to you. One very important thing to remember is to make sure your graphics are maximized to lessen the time it takes to open them. We've all been there, done that with slow-loading graphics, I'm sure. The professional web developer pays close attention to different platforms (Windows, Mac, Linux, Unix), different browsers (Internet Explorer, Netscape, WebTV), and different screen resolutions (newer monitors and laptops "see" things much differently than old monitors), and how all of those differences will affect the viewing of your writer's website.

Once you figure out who will build your website—you or a professional—you'll need to give careful consideration to your site's content. Here's the bare minimum for an author's website:

- A bio.
- A list of your publications. (Include scans of the cover[s] of your book[s], a synopsis, and perhaps an excerpt or two. I scanned the first two pages of each of my children's books and devoted one page of my website to them.) Your writing is the reason your website visitors are there in the first place, so they ought to be able to sample a page or two, or at least a paragraph.
- Positive feedback or reviews.
- Information on appearances and upcoming promotional events.
- Where your book can be found and ordering details.
- Your contact information.

Having made sure you've covered these essentials, the next step is to think about how to make a visit to your website enjoyable, educational, instructional, or fun. What makes your writer's website stand out from the thousands of others on the Internet? If you write children's books, how about adding a game page, or a start-your-own-story page, or come up with a contest for kids to enter to win a free copy of your book? If you make school appearances, kids will be checking out your website, so why not, at the very least, give them a place where they can make comments, or send you story ideas? If you have the capabilities and know-how, why not link to an audio file of you reading an excerpt from your book? The best way to figure out how to make your website interesting is to check out other authors' sites, and borrow workable ideas from them. During the writing of this chapter, I checked out John Grisham's and Michael Crichton's official websites. I figured they were household names in the book biz, and thought their sites would serve as good representative writers' websites. And they were very good and very sophisticated. I came away knowing a lot more about Michael Crichton than I knew before. We can also assume that their budgets for building a website were robust. Still, we writers on the lower rungs can take a clue from them about what's interesting information, and what's not.

Your website should reflect who you are, without an excessive foray into personal information that may be irrelevant to selling your book (pictures that take forever to load of you and your family at the Cape, endless paragraphs about your pet dog, Flash, or nattering on and on about your porcelain penguin collection). If you have something interesting to add about a location in your book, or a bit of lore about your setting or characters, share it with your visitors. They arrived at your site primarily to learn more about you, the author, and about the shared experience they've had reading your book.

Another possibility for inclusion in your website might be to keep an online journal. Perhaps you have some essays or short stories you could post that can act as a bonus treat for your visitors. If they arrive at your website because they've read one of your books, you must have left them wanting more, so give it to them. Why not talk about the process of writing for you, personally. When do you like to write? Does writing come easily to you, or is it a chore? How do you get your story ideas? What do you do when you suffer from writer's block? Or *do* you suffer from writer's block? What's your favorite book? Perhaps you can provide your visitors with a list of your favorite authors. Revealing the books and authors that you enjoy can often reveal a lot about yourself.

Once the site's up and running, keep it current so it doesn't start to have a dated, neglected air about it. Check your links regularly to make sure they still work. There's nothing more discouraging than clicking on a dead link.

And last but not least, publicize, publicize, publicize your website. Think of your website as a commercial product or an advertising tool. Like fertilizer, your website address won't do anyone any good unless it's spread around.

GLORIA D. HEINEMANN

48

Commercial Freelancing

Is It for You?

You love to write, and you'd love to write more, but a person has to earn a living. You've had several opinion essays published in the local newspaper and one in a small national magazine. Oh yes, you write on the job, but that's different: you'd like to have more control over what you write.

If you enjoy simplifying prose to readable copy, creating memorable slogans and headlines, learning about businesses, and helping companies put their best foot forward, then commercial freelance writing, sometimes called "copywriting," can help you. Writing for corporations and businesses can provide stability to a writer's income. Clients are out there, and they pay well. Most skills learned in this arena are directly applicable to other types of writing—for editors at major newspapers and magazines, literary agents, and publishing houses. Alternatively, you might find that you enjoy commercial freelancing so much that you want to devote more of your time to it.

Downsizing and outsourcing continue in business and industry today.

These trends have created a market for self-employed commercial writers, and given the lack of writing ability among many college graduates, there is an even greater demand for good commercial writers. Large, high-status companies in metropolitan areas tend to pay more than those in small, less-populated ones. If you live in a small market, however, you're not limited to a mediocre income. With modern technology, you can market yourself to companies located anywhere. Commercial writers make between $40 and $100 an hour. They usually charge clients a flat rate project rate or an hourly rate, which includes not only writing time, but also time in meetings and phone conversations, traveling to and from meetings, and time spent reading, researching, conceptualizing, brainstorming, and editing.

As you learn to market companies, you also learn to market yourself more effectively. You'll improve your ability to attract additional clients as well as sell ideas and articles to newspaper, magazine, and book editors via query and cover letters, phone conversations, and in person. Commercial freelancing creates the opportunity to learn about graphic design and to team up with a graphic designer on projects for end-to-end solutions for your clients, and these collaborative efforts afford additional opportunities for new clients. Working with clients in specific industries such as health, finance, or education can launch your writing in other directions—feature articles about fitness, budgeting, adult education, or public versus private education for children. Conversely, writing features in a specialty area can open doors for commercial writing as well.

Developing headlines or slogans or brainstorming themes gets your creative juices flowing for all types of writing. Preparing focused and concise copy for marketing brochures helps improve your writing ability. You'll hold the readers attention more effectively by eliminating unnecessary words and those complex, three and four syllable ones. Face-to-face interactions at business events help develop your interpersonal skills, so essential when meeting other writers and editors at local writers' groups, book signings, and professional writers' seminars and conferences.

What do you need to get started? Initially, you need a business card, a website, a telephone and computer, and a list of potential clients—companies that might hire you. Start with the yellow pages of your phone book and chamber of commerce or local business directories. Use the Internet to identify the names and contact information of persons in a company's marketing or communications department. Display examples of your work and excerpts from your work on your website. If you don't have a website, you'll need a portfolio with examples of your work to show to potential clients. If you're new to commercial writing, use brochures, newsletters, or manuals you've created at your workplace or as a volunteer with a nonprofit or professional organization. Otherwise do some "pro bono" marketing work or create "mock-up" examples (a press release, letters, and brochure) for your portfolio to show clients what they can expect from you. Remember you're not a graphic designer; your examples should "show off" your writing. As you build your writing business, you might want to purchase a fax and copy machine for increased efficiency and convenience.

How do you start? You start by making contacts to let the business world know you're out there. You need to build up a client and potential client database and continue to market yourself to these companies. It's best to start with what you know; so select companies in industries familiar to you. Educators might contact school systems, colleges, universities, and adult education programs in the community. Given modern technology, a variety of contact options are available to you. These include cold calls (your very first contact with a company), warm calls (a contact after a previous introduction), direct mail, e-mail, fax, postcards, and ads in relevant publications.

Regardless of which option or combination of options you use, the key is to follow up either by scheduling a face-to-face meeting or referring the potential client to your website. Many commercial writers send out creative marketing postcards on a regular basis throughout the year to potential clients in their database. And don't expect immediate results or be "put off" if someone tells you they already have a copywriter. Keep your name out there so they don't forget you.

If you think you might want to try commercial writing, there's someone you must meet. His name is Peter Bowerman (www.wellfedwriter.com), a very successful commercial freelancer and author of two "how to" books about writing for business clients. In his books *The Well-Fed Writer* and its following volume, *The Well-Fed Writer: Back for Seconds,* published in 2005 by Fanove Publishing, Peter takes you, step by step, through the process of becoming a self-sufficient commercial writer in six months or less. Peter injects just the right amount of humor to make reading these books both motivational and enjoyable. He opens up the business world to readers and gives them the tools to navigate through it. In the first book, he focuses on his own experiences learning to become a commercial writer. In the second, he includes the experiences of other commercial freelancers in his network.

In a phone conversation with Peter, I asked him for some tips for beginning commercial writers. His response includes:

- Remember that it's not that difficult to break into or transition into commercial freelancing.
- Think like a businessperson, not like a writer.
- Don't put companies on a pedestal; you have the skills to help them.
- Start small and work up.
- Start with what you know.
- Know your audience—your client's company and its potential customers.
- Think strategically; know what the company does best and highlight it in your writing.

Peter acknowledged that there is a misconception about commercial freelancing—that you have to "sell your soul" to sell marketing copy. While you do "work for hire" and don't retain copyright or receive a byline, you are helping companies present their best qualities, services, and products to their potential customers. When you do a good job for them, you'll be well compensated financially and valued and appreciated as a professional.

Once you become established as a commercial writer, you won't have to work forty to sixty hours per week. You can work on your own schedule and wear what you want when you write. If you want to make more money, you can take on additional clients or increase your rates. If you want to start that novel or that memoir, you can schedule your work so you have time for it. In commercial writing, it's up to you. You're in charge.

KATHRYN HELING

AND DEBORAH HEMBROOK

49

A Community of Writers

As educators, we're fond of saying "It takes a village . . ." and indeed we often find ourselves in collaboration with others. Routine activities—team teaching, faculty committees, planning sessions—provide daily opportunities for information sharing with professional peers.

Not so for the beginning writer, who is rarely lucky enough to have this type of ready-made network.

Completing your story or article marks only the first tiny step in a complicated process that can be confusing, frustrating, and lengthy. As you set out to get your words into print, you may soon find yourself a stranger in the strange (and often lonely) land of the writer.

A beginning writer faces more questions than answers. Is there a market for my work? Is my story more appropriate for a book or a magazine? How exactly do I go about submitting my writing to a publisher?

Fortunately, there are many resources available to assist you through this stage of "unconscious incompetence" and start you on the road to publication.

The *Children's Writer's and Illustrator's Market* (*CWIM*) is one such resource. Updated each year, the *CWIM* provides writers with a comprehensive listing of publishers of books, magazines, games, puzzles, and plays. The book is organized by genre and an alphabetical list of publishers within each genre. Educators may be especially interested in listings coded to indicate that the publisher produces educational material.

Each publisher's listing provides an overview of basic information regarding the current needs and interests of that particular company. Often, the listing will include the number of books published each year, what percent of those books were written by first-time authors, and names of books recently published by that company. You will find general guidelines for submitting work to the publisher, but you will want to check the publisher's website for more complete submission guidelines. Doing your homework is time well spent in helping to find a publisher that might be a good match for your work.

The *CWIM* also contains articles on a variety of topics of interest to the beginning or experienced writer. From practical advice on formatting your manuscript to state-of-the-craft guidelines for revisions, there's lots to learn in every edition. The *CWIM* is available through libraries, for purchase online, and in bookstores.

The annual updates of resource books such as the *CWIM* are an attempt to ensure that information is current; however, frequent changes in the world of children's literature are commonplace. Editors shift jobs, moving from one publishing company to another, and editorial policies may change as a result. For example, some publishers will not accept unsolicited or unagented work; other publishers accept manuscripts only during certain months of the year; and still others want you to send a query letter instead of a manuscript. If you are serious about becoming a published author, it is important to keep abreast of market changes and submission guidelines. When you send a talking animal story to a publisher that only publishes nonfiction, you quickly mark yourself as an amateur, someone who has not adequately researched the market.

Anyone aspiring to write for children should consider joining the Society for Children's Book Writers and Illustrators (SCBWI). The SCBWI is an international organization and an important informational network for people involved in publishing for children. The scbwi.org website offers a few articles and helpful tips for free, but mostly provides information and links for members only. The website makes it easy to join on-line. Whether you are an SCBWI member or not, you are able to access on-line information regarding regional events, thereby getting an indication of the types of SCBWI activities for writers in your area.

Upon joining the SCBWI, you will receive a new member packet of publications providing you with an excellent overview of all aspects of writing for children. How do you write an effective cover letter to accompany your submission? What does it mean if the publisher asks for a "query"? Can you submit your manuscript to more than one publisher at a time? Through these introductory materials, you will learn about publishers, agents, various markets, educational programs, contracts, critique groups, editorial services, and more. Bimonthly SCBWI bulletins keep you apprised of market trends and the types of submissions that publishers would like to see. If an editor moves from one publishing house to another, or editorial policies change, you will be spared the wasted time and postage of sending an inappropriate submission.

Throughout the year, SCBWI conferences and writer's workshops are held at the international, national, and regional level. As an SCBWI member, you receive preferential notification and discounted registration fees for these conferences. Conference formats run the gamut from a three-hour luncheon on a Saturday, to several days of intensive workshops led by recognized experts in the field of children's literature. When you attend a conference, you'll have the opportunity to talk with writers at all levels, ranging from those just getting started to those who are making their living as an author.

Beyond the camaraderie, attendance at a writer's conference can provide invaluable contacts with editors. It's very common for editors to be among the speakers at a conference. Often, these editors represent well-known publishing companies that are "closed" to unsolicited manuscripts; in other words, they accept agented material only, and beginning writers rarely have an agent. Editors appreciate that writers in attendance at conferences are serious about their craft, and those editors will almost always offer a specific window of time during which writers in attendance are invited to submit a manuscript to the publisher. In this way, writers have been able to "break into" publishing companies that would have been otherwise completely off-limits to them.

So . . . you've joined the SCBWI and studied the new member materials with the zeal of someone cramming for a final examination. You've highlighted entire sections of the *CWIM*. You've attended a conference or two and connected with other writers who, like you, are striving to make their dream of becoming a published author a reality. You've created what you truly believe to be charming stories, sending them only to publishers whose interests seem a good match for your talents. But time after time, your submission is returned with a form letter:

> *Dear Author . . .*
> *After careful consideration of your work . . .*
> *Not right for our list . . .*
> *Blah, blah, blah . . .*

In the all-too-frequent absence of informational feedback to accompany the rejection, you are left to wonder . . . was there anything worthwhile about my story? What was good? What was not so good? What can I do to fix it?

Many writers find help with such questions by joining a critique group. Critique groups vary in their "personalities" as much as the members that comprise them. A critique group usually consists of about six members, willing to share what they've written and to offer supportive and constructive criticism to each other. Some critique group members live across country from one another, meeting only on-line. Other groups gather in person, having met through a writing class or at a conference.

In some critique groups, all the members focus on one genre, such as young adult novels. In other groups, diverse writing interests result in a healthy mix of opinions and ideas. Guidelines for forming and maintaining effective critique groups are found in the *CWIM* and through the SCBWI, or by asking advice from existing groups.

If all this information whets your appetite for more, there are several books that would make the start of an excellent resource library. A few of the more notable include:

- *What's Your Story* by Marion Dane Bauer. The subtitle of this book reads *A Young Person's Guide to Writing Fiction,* but don't let that turn you away. Chapter by chapter, you will be lead through the essential steps of creating a story.
- *Bird by Bird* by Anne Lamott instructs the aspiring writer

through valuable "how-to's" embedded in the hilarious context of life as a writer.

- Olga Litowinsky's *It's a Bunny-Eat-Bunny World* advertises itself as *A Writer's Guide to Surviving and Thriving in Today's Competitive Children's Book Market.* The first part of the book is a fascinating history of children's publishing, while the remainder gives the reader helpful insights into negotiating the publishing process in today's market.

There are other excellent on-line resources for writers in addition to the scbwi.org website. Write4kids.com offers helpful free-access information in addition to the option of subscribing to a newsletter and additional members-only on-line resources. The Purple Crayon at underdown.org offers a wealth of free information related to all aspects of writing, illustrating, and publishing children's books.

You may be fortunate to live in an area in which courses geared toward writing for children are offered. Aside from honing your craft, attendance at classes offers you yet another venue for connecting with fellow writers.

Whatever your level or nature of interest in writing for children, it's hard to go it alone. If you work with children, you already have the advantage of constant contact with your targeted audience. You can give yourself an even greater edge toward your goal of publishing if you take an active role in educating yourself in all aspects of the writing and publishing process. When you create your own "village," your writing community, you'll have a support system beyond the solitary butt-in-chair time that writing requires. You'll have someone to commiserate with when the story just won't come together, someone to cry with when the rejections pile up, and someone who understands the significance of your accomplishment when your name *finally* appears on a published piece.

PATRICIA A. PARRISH

50

Designing Action Research

A Brief Guide to Why and How

Teachers are often perplexed by the phenomenon they experience in their classrooms. There are times when "scientifically based approaches" may not be leading to the student growth that was promised, or when classroom management seems to be interfering with the academic focus desired by the teacher. Addressing these phenomena through action research can provide a teacher with data that can be used as a foundation for a research publication. This chapter will explore the fundamentals of action research, including process, dealing with human subject protection, and sharing research results.

When faced with classroom dilemmas, teachers often feel a sense of cognitive dissonance (Festinger, 1964; 1965), or a mismatch between their beliefs and their experiences. As teachers become more proactive in their professional practice, they are motivated to find out "why" experiences and beliefs are not aligned. One way a teacher can do this is by engaging in a new type of research: a teacher-directed, teacher-motivated type of research that leads to the answers the teacher needs. This is action research.

There are many topics a teacher could address through action research. Anytime a teacher feels an approach she is using in the classroom could be improved, she has the opportunity to engage in action research. Some examples of appropriate questions for an action research project include (but are not limited to):

- Is a new teaching strategy being implemented effectively for this group of students?
- Does a particular student struggle with an academic or behavioral area that is being targeted for improvement?
- How can classroom transition times be made more efficient?
- How can computers be incorporated effectively into daily classroom routines?

Many times a teacher will recognize the need to gather data regarding an issue in her classroom, but will not engage in research because of a concern that it is too complicated. Anyone who has taken a research methods course is familiar with the concept of generalizing results. In order to conduct traditional research, it is necessary to be sure that the research design accounts for reliability, internal validity, and external validity. This means factors need to be controlled that could prevent the results from being applied in new settings (Stringer, 2004). This is a critical component of traditional research and cannot be discounted. However, in action research, the purpose is for a teacher to try new strategies and to determine if they are working in her classroom. There is no desire to generalize to other settings, so it is unnecessary to be concerned with external validity or with a false sense of objectivity (Holly et al., 2005; Stringer, 2004). Action research is as much about professional development as it is about research; that is what makes it such an appealing approach.

If action research is not about generalization and focuses as much on professional development as it does on "knowledge," why would the results be publishable? The answer to this is based on value. Oftentimes as teachers we share a dilemma with others in hopes of getting ideas on how to address it. Even if the solutions offered do not work, we feel better knowing we are not alone. Humans value knowing others face similar dilemmas and value knowing how someone else responded. Action research serves the professional nunity by providing information on what issues are being faced by others and how they are being handled. If a teacher has gone to the effort of systematically exploring a phenomenon, her findings will be of interest to other teachers, even if the specific results are not generalized. The solution that works for you as an action researcher may work for another. Sharing your new-found knowledge will help others improve their practice.

When conducting research, whether traditional or action, a teacher is expected to abide by three ethical principles: respect for people, beneficences, and justice. Basically, this means the teacher will need to ensure no participants will be harmed, that the benefits of the intended research outweigh the risks, and that all parties are treated fairly (Skarbek et al., in press). In order to ensure that the proposed research meets these ethical standards, many school districts and all universities have a process in place to review research before it is conducted. This process is called human subject protection. Before beginning an action research project, it is a good idea for a teacher to check with the local school district to find out if a human subject protection review is required. If no review is required, it would be wise for the teacher to share plans with the building administrator to ensure support in completing the project.

Once you have a research question and any needed permissions to conduct your action research, it is time to design your project. During this stage of action research, you will focus your question on what you really want to learn or to know. Part of this process is reviewing the literature to see what is already known about your topic. You will also want to identify the assumptions and biases you have toward your research topic, as these are likely to influence the way you conduct research (Holly et al., 2005). Next, you will decide specifically on the changes you plan to make in your classroom and how you will collect data to document the impact of the changes. Your data collection and analysis techniques do not need to be complex. They can be as simple as comparing scores on a pre-test to scores on a post-test for issues related to academic achievement, timing the amount of time students need to complete a transition between activities if you are trying to improve transitions in your classroom, or counting the number of student call-outs during a lesson if you are concerned about classroom management. Once these issues are decided, you are ready to begin collecting data. If as you conduct your research you find your data collection technique is not providing the information you need, it is acceptable to change it.

Once you gather your data, you will need to analyze them. This can be done with simple statistics or with qualitative interpretation. The goal is to see if the changes you made had the impact you desired. If so, you have been successful in solving your problem. If not, you will want to reflect more and determine another strategy!

Once the research has been completed, you will want to find a way to share your results. This can be done informally by sharing with a friend or through a presentation to the faculty at your school. More formal methods include a paper presentation at a conference or through the publication of an article based on your research. Naturally, for those hoping to develop a professional vita, the formal methods are desirable.

A well-designed, ethically implemented action research project is a great way for a teacher to not only have writing opportunities, but also it is an excellent way to hone and advance professional skills to improve teaching skills and ultimately student achievement.

References

Festinger, L. (1964). *Conflict, Decision, and Dissonance.* Stanford, CA: Stanford University Press.

Festinger, L. (1965). *A Theory of Cognitive Dissonance.* Stanford, CA: Stanford University Press.

Holly, M. L., Arhar, J. & Kasten, W. (2005). *Action Research for Teachers: Traveling the Yellow Brick Road,* 2nd edn. Upper Saddle River, NJ: Pearson Education.

Skarbek, D. M., Henry, P. & Parrish, P. A. (2006 March/April). The Institutional Review Board: Another major ingredient of our alphabet soup. *Teaching Exceptional Children* 38(4), 26-30..

Stringer, E. (2004). *Action Research in Education.* Upper Saddle River, NJ: Pearson Education.

M. D. OSBORNE

51

The Educational Support Materials Writer

Writer or Educator?

Teachers teach; students learn. At least that's what we assume takes place inside classrooms all over the country, and, indeed, all over the world. Teaching students to think, widely agreed to be *the* goal of education, is a tough job. But can all that supposed learning be measured? The first thing that might spring to mind when assessment of classroom learning is mentioned is probably that nasty, four-letter word: TEST. Yes, that beloved beast, the test. That process we hope adequately measures a student's ability to remember and reproduce what was presented to him by an instructor over a certain period of time. Let's take a brief look at how and why these tests are created, and who creates them.

What are the ingredients used in making a test? One place to begin is by defining the nature of thinking. Much research has been made into *how* students learn. Before we can begin to make learning better, or assess it, we need to know more of what it is. In 1956, Benjamin Bloom created a taxonomy (simply a means of classification) that serves as the basis for what are now called higher-order thinking skills. (Bloom was the first name listed in alphabetical order of so many editors that they became the ubiquitous "and others" of a taxonomy developed by a large committee of people.) This model included six levels of thinking: knowledge, comprehension, application, analysis, synthesis and evaluation, and is sometimes represented as a pyramid, with knowledge as the broad base of the pyramid. Educators have long used this structure to build curriculum materials that take learners more deeply into any area of study. However, there are certain researchers and educators who don't think the taxonomy fills the total bill. You may be a dyed-in-the-wool supporter of Benjamin Bloom's higher-order thinking, or you may find his taxonomy's pyramid a bit bottom-heavy and unwieldy to serve as a suitable map of the typical student's cognitive terrain.

But, however you feel about the hows, whys and driving forces behind student learning, assessment tools and diagnostic materials designed to measure learning are constantly being created. Providing educational support materials has become a booming business, one that is waiting for you, the educator, to join its ranks.

If you run an Internet search for "educational assessment tools" you will find a veritable banquet of sites hawking their wares, offering one-stop shopping for these professional tools. But, have you ever wondered who writes these things? Standardized tests like the ACT and SAT are written by everyday educators who are "committed to improving education around the world" and in helping "teachers help their students learn" (quoted directly from the ETS website, producers of the SAT). The ACT test questions are written by people from a variety of backgrounds, many of whom are high school teachers themselves. These writing jobs usually require a minimum of a four-year degree at an accredited college or university, and almost always prefer that the candidates have strong teaching experience. Some companies that provide tests to measure the completion of a learning task—as in, say, the reading of a book—may hire people with standard four-year degrees who have a variety of backgrounds such as chemistry, history, English, literature, education, a foreign language, etc., in order to provide a diverse bouquet of experts.

Most of these tests strive to provide concise, clear questions on subjects that are pleasant and uncontroversial. Test publishing companies and individual states dictate which topics are considered "safe" for their writers to use when creating questions or story samples for standardized tests. Certain subjects are held to be taboo (subjects that may be inappropriate or potentially upsetting to children like death, violence, drugs or sex), and a list of banned words that should be avoided at all costs is also provided to writers. So, if you're a hotheaded, maverick educator/writer who longs to write that barrier-breaking Great American Standardized Test, then you'll probably want to stick to classroom teaching, or choose to write the Great American Novel instead. In fact, one of the things standardized test writers may have in common is that they are corralled into writing the same kinds of questions with the same, general content as all other writers who work within their company. Ideally, no one test should stand out as either more stellar or lousier than another. Once these tests are written and edited (a meticulous process that is quite a feat in and of itself), they undergo some sort of field testing to weed out questions that are too easy or too hard, and/or those that may stump particular groups of students.

There have been many instances in which a private company that now provides these assessment tools was started by an educator who was frustrated because he or she longed to have well-written, thought-provoking materials to use in the classroom. If you don't have the stamina or wherewithal to start your own company, there are plenty of companies and agencies out there looking for educators turned writers for hire. You won't get rich. You'll have plenty of deadlines to meet. You may feel straight jacketed at times because of trying to please the topic- and banned-word police. You may feel daunted by having to create a "product" for sale, something foreign and daunting to most classroom educators. But, you won't find this profession boring, since the material to be covered is usually varied and interesting. And, if you keep in mind the student who will ultimately take the test you've crafted with care, you'll no doubt find it gratifying as well.

SAMUEL TOTTEN

52

Endless Topics to Write About

Local, State, Regional, National, and International Social Issues

Social issues abound. Most are controversial. The latter is due to the fact that people with vastly different political beliefs and values often view the issues in radically different ways. Even what some may consider to be fairly innocuous issues (e.g., a town ordinance requiring all bicyclists to wear helmets, city ordinances mandating recycling of papers and bottles, the establishment of charter schools) have the power to raise hackles. The most controversial (e.g., abortion, the threat of nuclear war, the death penalty, gun control, book banning, citywide smoking bans, affirmative action, merit pay for teachers) are capable of generating fierce debate, intense lobbying, and, in some cases, civil disobedience. The point is, the discussion, debate, and examination of social issues are ripe topics for writers. Indeed, those who are interested in social issues have a wealth of possibilities for getting their thoughts and words in print—from letters to the editor to guest editorials in local and regional newspapers, and from articles in educational journals (e.g., *Harvard*

Educational Review, Teachers College Record, Educational Leadership, Social Education, The Social Studies, Journal of Environmental Education, English Journal, Theory and Research in Social Education) to articles in activist magazines (e.g., *Bulletin of Atomic Scientists, Society, The Progressive, Southern Exposure, Sojourners*), and popular magazines (e.g., *Atlantic Monthly* or *The New York Times Magazine*). Additional outlets are chapters in edited books, the editing of a book on social issues (and/or educating about social issues), and even single-authored books.

Selecting an issue to write about is as simple as what one is interested in, irritated by, concerned with, or frightened over. Over the years, for example, I have written letters to the editor voicing my support for a citywide ban on smoking, and I've also written numerous guest editorials for both state and local newspapers on the subject of the ongoing genocide in Darfur, Sudan. Educational journals have been a reliable source of publication for my articles on such topics as the deprivation of human rights, the need for a total ban on smoking on public school grounds, the danger of the nuclear arms race, and various aspects of genocides. I've also written scores of essays on many of the aforementioned topics for scholarly journals and edited volumes, and I've served as the editor and co-editor of a dozen books on various social issues. The point is, if one has an interest in a "hot" or controversial social issue, one is likely to find an outlet for one's thoughts and words.

As with any writing assignment, one of the first things an author writing about a particularly social issue must do is decide on his/her target audience. That will invariably influence the voice and length of the piece, as well as where the piece is submitted for publication. Obviously, one's tone is going to be quite, if not radically, different if he/she is planning to submit an article to *The Radical Teacher* (a socialist, feminist, and anti-racist journal on the theory and practice of teaching) versus *The American Educator* (a publication with a decidedly more conservative take on the world).

One of the many joys of writing about social issues is that writing with "voice" almost comes naturally, and that is even true for the most scholarly of pieces. I believe that is true due to the fact that when one writes about which one is passionate, one's voice naturally, and powerfully, comes to the fore.

A certain amount of knowledge, of course, is needed to write about a social issue. The requisite depth of knowledge, though, is contingent on where one is published. If one, for example, is writing an opinion piece for inclusion in a newspaper, one certainly must get his/her facts right, but he/she is not expected to have nearly the expertise and nuanced understanding of an issue as one who is publishing in a scholarly journal.

When possible, it is generally a good idea to use quotes from various sources that support one's position. In doing so, though, it is imperative to quote those who are considered *the* experts in the field, and are highly respected. Conversely, it is wise to avoid quoting those who are considered "off the wall" or "quacks." Using quotes from the latter totally undermine one's argument.

Educational journals are a great venue for those who are just beginning to publish their work on social issues. Such journals are constantly in search of new and fresh voices who are writing on issues of concern to their readership. Furthermore, most educational journal editors are "writer friendly," and are actually willing to take the time and effort to shepherd a piece through the publication process if he/she sees merit in a piece. It is also much easier to place a piece in an educational journal than a scholarly journal or a popular magazine such as *Atlantic Monthly.*

On a different but related note, once an author has met with some success and becomes known as an "expert" on a particular social issue, many educational journals welcome proposals for special issues from authors. Over the past twenty years, for example, I have had the good fortune of editing or co-editing more than a half dozen special issues on a variety of social issues (e.g., the deprivation of human rights [*Social Education*]; horizontal nuclear proliferation [*Social Education*]; genocide [*Social Education*]; terrorism [*Social Science Record*]; the harmful effects of tobacco [*Social Science Record*]; and even a special issue on teaching about social issues for the *Arizona English Bulletin*).

Finally, there is not only something extremely satisfying about publishing an article on a social issue, but also getting one's voice and views out into the larger world where they become part of the larger dialog around an issue. The ultimate sense of satisfaction comes, if it does, when your ideas are picked up and commented on elsewhere and/or used, even if in part, to help solve a problem.

PATRICIA A. PARRISH

53

Multicultural Education's Place in Educational Writing

Multicultural education has become a buzzword in many educational circles. While most educators recognize the need to develop a multicultural perspective, many are not certain what this means or how to incorporate this important topic into their writing. This will provide an overview of multicultural education, ways to include multicultural perspectives into educational writing and how to avoid unintentionally marginalizing readers from heritage cultures.

Multicultural education grew out of the civil rights movement of the 1960s (Nieto, 1996) and is described as a reform movement (Banks, 2002). Multicultural education is concerned with providing education in the context of a pluralistic approach to society, based on the idea that education should lead to social change and social justice (Sleeter, 1996). A classroom based on multiculturalism will value all cultures equally and will advocate for all students to understand and accept the many cultures found in our society.

As our nation grows and welcomes people from many countries around the world, our population dynamics continue to change. Results of the 2000 US Census indicate that 75.1% of the population listed themselves as White and 12.3% of the population considers themselves to be Black or African American (US Census Bureau, 2000). Additionally, 12.5% of the population listed their cultural heritage as Hispanic or Latino (US Census Bureau, 2000). It is important to note that Hispanic or Latino heritage is not a racial classification as are White or Caucasian and Black or African American (Grieko & Cassidy, 2000). The population of the United States is constantly increasing in diversity, so it is projected that only 59% of school-aged children will be White, non-Hispanic by 2010 (McDevitt & Ormrod, 2004). Within some states the population is expected to become majority-minority within the next ten years. This means that while White people will still be the largest population category, they will make up less than 50% of the total population.

As our population becomes more and more diverse, teachers need to modify instructional approaches and educational expectations to fit their students. This will naturally impact how and why we write as educators. Including this multicultural perspective can become a way of life, but it takes openness to change and willingness to see the world from a perspective different from your own.

Another concept that is related to multicultural education is marginalization. When a group is marginalized, it means they are pushed to the outside of a social circle, to the margins of the circle. This happens when a group is forced to choose between giving up a piece of their culture or being rejected from mainstream culture because of it. It also happens when one group's perception of others pushes them away from social acceptance, even if the perception is inaccurate (Banks, 2002).

As teachers engage in the writing process, we must recognize that we are bound within our individual culture. While it is not possible, nor is it desirable, to remove ourselves from our culture, we must recognize that our culture influences our interpretation of events and of data. We also must recognize that a desired outcome in our personal culture might not be desired in other cultures. A simple example of this is a middle-class teacher of Western European decent who expects children to look her in the eye when she is speaking. This is a common cultural expectation for many of us, but for children from some cultures it is considered disrespectful to look a person of authority in the eye. Engaging in a battle of wills, by demanding a child look at you when you are speaking, can actually be counterproductive. Rather, we need to recognize the cultural difference and accept the child's comfort level and belief system. Is our goal truly to have the child look at us or to have the child listen to us?

This example can be applied to writing as well. When a teacher is explaining his practice or his research, he needs to be aware that what works in his classroom with the students from the cultural heritage(s) in his community might not work, or even be desirable, for those from other classrooms. That does not devalue the work he has done, but he must also recognize that it does not devalue the culture of other communities. Often, researchers have marginalized readers by inferring that one culture is somehow preferable to another, or that certain cultural customs are inappropriate. It is better to recognize that different environments have different expectations. What is expected in a classroom may vary from what is expected at home. This does not make the home wrong; it merely makes the home different. When writing for publication, it is critical to keep this in mind and to accept all cultures as equal. Then, from this perspective to explain how a behavior, learning strategy, or classroom expectation is desirable within a specific environment.

Another important aspect of adopting a multicultural perspective is to keep in mind that not all people of common descent will share the same cultural expectations. One family of Hispanic descent may still speak Spanish in the home and celebrate traditional holidays of their heritage country. Another family of Hispanic decent may have adopted the culture of the White, American middle class and never speak Spanish in the home. The children of these families are unique, and should not be expected to have the same outward expression of cultural heritage. As writers, we must be careful not to assign cultural expectations based only on race or heritage. We must evaluate each situation and each student based on the context of our interaction.

When writing from a multicultural perspective, educators must avoid stereotypical statements while valuing the many different cultures that exist within the United States. When describing students, it is important to include information on culture and race; but it is inappropriate to use that as the only defining information. If uncertain how your writing might be received by members of a specific heritage or cultural group, it is a good idea to ask a member of the group for input. As long as educators recognize the need to adopt a multicultural perspective, along with the need to decenter and avoid marginalizing groups of people, their writing can have the desired impact without offending readers.

References

Banks, J. A. (2002). *An Introduction to Multicultural Education,* 3rd edn. Boston: Allyn and Bacon.

Grieko, E. M. & Cassidy, R. C. (2000). *Census 2000 Brief: Overview of Race and Hispanic Origin.* Washington, DC: United States Census Bureau.

McDevitt, T. M. & Ormrod, J. (Eds.) (2004). *Child Development: Educating and Working with Children and Adolescents,* 2nd edn. Upper Saddle River, NJ: Pearson Prentice Hall.

Nieto, S. (1996). *Affirming Diversity: The Sociopolitical Context of Multicultural Education,* 2nd edn. White Plains, NY: Longman.

Sleeter, C. E. (1996). *Multicultural Education as Social Activism.* Albany, NY: State University of New York Press.

United States Census Bureau (2000) United States Census 2000. Washington, DC.

ANN DIXON

54

Surviving and Thriving as a Visiting Author

Every writer travels a unique path to publication. Whether you write picture books or poetry, science fiction or nonfiction, audiences in schools and libraries are interested in learning what *you've* learned along the way. By presenting programs as a visiting author you can synthesize your passions for writing and teaching, while also interacting with your audience, promoting your work, and augmenting your income.

Planning Presentations

The first step is a personal inventory. What unique interests, information, skills, experiences, and perspectives have you gained as a writer? If you've become an authority on a topic through writing about it, put together a presentation. Include information that didn't make it into publication and perhaps discuss how you made those editing decisions. This kind of "insider" information will intrigue those who've already read your work and motivate those who haven't to do so. Other potential topics may arise from the creative process, as well as the technical aspects involved in researching, writing, editing, illustrating, and publishing.

Next, brainstorm a list of special skills. Can you incorporate music, drama, art, or other talents into your program? For example, I often tell, rather than read, my story *Blueberry Shoe* and then discuss aspects of the picture book page by page. Teachers and students alike seem to appreciate this dual approach to literature.

For school visits, think about ways to relate your materials to educational curriculum and standards. To accomplish this you'll need to consider the age of your audience, which also affects their attention span, interests, and skills.

Some writers are terrified at the thought of facing preschoolers, while others blanch at the prospect of teens. If you're not sure which age groups you prefer, first try working with various ages as a volunteer. Don't be afraid to step out of your comfort zone, but do prepare thoughtfully. Will your topic interest all ages, or only some? Can you present the same topic to everyone by varying your methods, or not? Can age levels be combined? For example, a different approach is needed to present poetry to first graders with emerging writing skills than to fluent sixth graders. It might work to combine grades one and two, and grades five and six, but not one and six.

In addition to age, consider length of presentation, group size, and setting. Forty-five to sixty minutes with older children is a realistic guideline but may be too long for younger students. I usually limit my preschool program, for instance, to thirty minutes. For hands-on or workshop projects, more time is usually needed.

Group size can range from large assemblies to mid-sized groups of three or four classes to individual classroom workshops. Larger groups may make it possible to include all students if funding is limited, but will reduce the options for hands-on activities and personal interaction. Be realistic and clear about your preferences. A sixty-minute session on researching nonfiction may work well in class-sized groups, but can you pull it off if several classes are combined? Large-group presentations require a degree of stage presence, comfort with microphones, and strategies for holding the interest of students in the back row of a multi-purpose room with terrible acoustics.

Group size often determines the setting. Generally, the more intimate the setting, the better. Disruptions such as lunch preparations, classes shuffling past, and worst of all, recess can foil a presenter's most enchanting spell. Perhaps the library can accommodate larger groups, or maybe a room divider is available to improve acoustics, block distractions, and create a cozier atmosphere in a multi-purpose room. Remember to modify your visual aids to suit the setting. For example, showing pages from your book may work fine in a classroom, but in an auditorium you'll need to project the images.

Preparing

Use your lesson-planning skills to prepare a program that not only interests children, but also generates enthusiasm for reading, writing, and learning. Make an outline, devise activities, gather your visual aids, and then practice. Time yourself repeatedly until you are completely comfortable with your presentation. Anticipate glitches, such as technology failures, interruptions, or changes in schedule.

You can help the teachers, as well as yourself, by creating standards-based activity guides that tie your books to the curriculum. A one- or two-page flyer will not only be appreciated, but also keep your book in demand.

Communicate with the coordinator of your visit, usually a teacher or librarian, well ahead of time. Work out the details of age grouping, audience sizes, scheduling, and setting. Request microphones, projectors, or other technology you may need and plan on arriving early to make sure the equipment is working. Also discuss other items, such as activity materials, a whiteboard, podium, easel, table, or chair.

Determine whether or not you will be autographing books. If so, who will supply them? Make sure the books are ordered in time for arrival.

Last, but on my list not least, ask about lunch!

Presenting

Now it's time to relax and have fun. Here are some tips to help your presentation succeed:

- Incorporate audience participation, storytelling, learning activities, music, or visual aids, such as props, artifacts, or slides to hold your group's interest.

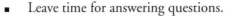

- Leave time for answering questions.
- Be aware of the schedule and stick to it. (You should have a copy.)
- Be flexible, but speak up if you need something.
- Ignore small interruptions. Recognize larger ones briefly before moving on.
- Require teacher attendance. (You are not a babysitter.)
- Ask for staff intervention if a situation becomes uncomfortable.
- Above all, let your enthusiasm for your topic shine through.

And Don't Forget . . . the Business

Few authors today make a living from the proceeds of their writing. Professional writers approach school and library appearances as an extension of their creative work, and as a business endeavor.

Getting the Word Out

Word of mouth, news releases about recent books or awards, interviews in local media, book signings, and recognition among other educators and librarians may lead to invitations to present. Speaking locally to groups you are familiar with is a good way to gain experience.

For a more proactive approach:

- Contact local or state arts councils, or the state education department, about applying to "artist in the schools" programs.
- Let your publisher know you are interested in author visits. They may receive requests.
- Check with writers' organizations in your area to see if a speaker listing exists.
- Create a flyer describing your presentations. Distribute it at signings, professional gatherings, libraries, and schools.
- Talk to parents, teachers, and librarians you know.
- Contact schools and libraries by telephone or by mailing your flyer to the principal, librarian, or reading instructor.

At some point you may want to create a website that includes information about your programs. There are also agencies that will list your information nationally. An Internet search for "author visits" will yield several. Be sure to inquire about fees.

Contracts

Some districts require that an agreement be signed before presenting. If not, it's a good idea to supply one to prevent misunderstandings. Obtain a boilerplate contract or create your own. (For a free example, see http://tonibuzzeo.com/visitcontracts.html, courtesy of Toni Buzzeo, author of the book *Terrific Connections with Authors, Illustrators and Storytellers*.) Specify the date, institution, payment, time of payment, expenses covered, number of sessions, responsibility for book sales, and other potentially problematic matters such as unexpected illness, cancellation fees, and permission to record. Be prepared to provide an invoice, as well.

Money

Many authors sometimes volunteer their services, especially during the early stages of learning their craft. However, you'll quickly discover how much time and energy is involved in preparing and presenting programs. Most writers cannot afford the loss of writing time without compensation. So, be professional and remember that professionals get paid. Expect compensation unless you are making a deliberate donation. If the terms are unclear, ask: "Are you inviting me to speak as a volunteer or as a paid presenter?"

How much should you charge? That depends on experience, number of books, popularity, locale, and your personal needs. Typical honorariums range from $300 to $1500 per day (or more) for well-known authors. Talk to other authors in your area and join the Society for Children's Book Writers and Illustrators (SCBWI) and consult their guidelines. Include expenses like travel, lodging, and meals, as well as the number and length of sessions in your deliberation. Be aware that some school districts have very tight budgets, but that grants are often available. Also, school-sponsored sales of your books can raise a portion or all of the funds needed. Learn about those possibilities so you can suggest them.

Resources

Joining the SCBWI (http://www.scbwi.org) will give you access to many useful publications, including sample contracts and tips for school visits. Toni Buzzeo's previously mentioned *Terrific Connections* and her website (http://tonibuzzeo.com/visits.html) are aimed at librarians and teachers but contain a great deal of information helpful for writers, as well. *The Complete Idiot's Guide to Publishing Children's Books,* by Harold Underdown, includes a section on author visits. You should also talk to other writers and visit author websites.

Finally, trust your own resources. As an educator, you already know how to create lesson plans for specific age, skill, and curriculum levels, as well as improvize when circumstances change. As a writer, you know how to create and communicate.

So plan, prepare, present, and relax. You're the visiting author!

Contributors

CYNTHIA BRACKETT-VINCENT holds a BFA in Creative Writing from the University of Maine at Farmington; publishes *The Aurorean, a Poetic Quarterly* (featured in *Poet's Market*); is an award-winning poet whose chapbook, *The 95 Poems,* was published in 2005. She lives in rural Maine, lectures on poetry publishing, offers workshops and Adult Education poetry classes.

SUZANNE L. BUNKERS, Professor of English, Minnesota State University, is the author of *In Search of Susanna: an Auto/biography,* edited *Diaries of Girls and Women: a Midwestern American Sampler* among others, co-edited, *Inscribing the Daily: Critical Essays on Women's Diaries,* and has published numerous articles.

SHARON CHMIELARZ has had thirty years teaching experience in the public schools. She's also a poet and writer in such works as: *The Rhubarb*

King, End of Winter, Pied Piper of Hamelin. She's received Minnesota State Arts Board and Jerome Foundation Fellowships. Her work has been nominated for the Pushcart Prize.

ANN DIXON, from Alaska, has written magazine articles, essays, and poetry for adults, as well as eight books for children, including *Big-Enough Anna* and *Blueberry Shoe.* She leads preschool Story Time at her local public library, is guest author and storyteller, and is completing a master's degree in library science.

CHARLES T. DORRIS is a freelance book editor in San Francisco. For more than ten years, he has worked with academicians on books about business, public policy, and personal development. Charles has degrees from Vanderbilt University and the University of Virginia.

GLORIA D. HEINEMANN is a Health Education Specialist, Director of Patient Health Education, and health care team expert/consultant at VA Western New York Healthcare System. She also is Clinical Assistant Professor in the Department of Medicine, University at Buffalo, SUNY. She co-edited/co-authored *Team Performance in Health Care: Assessment and Development* and has written numerous articles.

Co-authors **KATHRYN HELING** and **DEBORAH HEMBROOK** are colleagues in the School District of Waukesha in southeastern Wisconsin. Kathryn is a school psychologist and Deborah is a Kindergarten teacher. They have published three early phonics readers and one write-in reader with Random House and are under contract with Raven Tree Press for two picture books. They are also contributors to *Highlights for Children.*

LARRY LOEBELL is a screenwriter, playwright, and dramaturg who has taught play and screen writing for 20 years, currently in the Theater Department at Arcadia University in Glenside, PA. Produced full-length plays include *La Tempestad, The Ballad of John Wesley Reed,* and *Pride of the Lion.* Larry co-wrote and received EMMY recognition for *Incident in Aisle Seven.*

KATIE MCKY has taught K-12 for 23 years in Massachusetts, Ohio, and Wisconsin as well as adults at Harvard's Kennedy School of Government. She is a storyteller, columnist, and the author of *Tough Kids, Tough Classrooms, It All Began with a Bean,* the *Crazy Girl* reading series, *Wildchilds, Pumpkin*

Town, and approximately 100 magazine articles and essays.

MAGGIE MIESKE, a Dean's List honors student, will graduate from Central Michigan University with a Bachelor of Science: English major, Creative Writing Concentration and a Spanish minor and begin a TESOL Master's Program in 2006. Her poetry has appeared in *The Aurorean, Parnassus Literary Journal, Cotyledon,* and others.

GLORIA NIXON-JOHN is a teacher-educator, school consultant, contributor to such texts as: *Those Who Do, Can: Teachers Writing, Writers Teaching,* stories and poems in *The Dunes Review.* She is currently working on a memoir about growing up in Detroit, lyrics for an off Broadway musical, and the true story of the youngest person on death row in America.

M.D. OSBORNE, once an educator in a high-risk teen program, now works as a quiz writer for assessment tests used in schools throughout the United States. She also writes, illustrates and publishes books for children through Wooden Shoe Press, a publishing company she started. *The Boy Who Loved To Shim-Sham Shimmy* was published in 2005.

PATRICIA A. PARRISH is an Assistant Professor of Education at Saint Leo University in Saint Leo, Florida. She has contributed to several books including, *The Passion of Teaching: Dispositions in the Schools;* and *Bulletproof Vests vs. the Ethic of Care: Which Strategy is Your School Using?* and the journal of the Florida Association of Teacher Educators.

VON PITTMAN is Director of the Center for Distance and Independent Study at the University of Missouri-Columbia. He is a contributing editor to the *Journal of Continuing Higher Education* and the author of the "how-to" book, *Surviving Graduate School Part-Time.*

ANN RIEDLING, Associate Professor, Louisville, Kentucky, has served two Fulbright Scholarships in Bahrain and Oman. She has published textbooks and tradebooks such as *Learning to Learn.* Ann has presented locally, nationally and internationally regarding a number of library-related topics.

CAROL SMALLWOOD, teacher and librarian, has had seventeen books published such as *Michigan Authors, An Educational Guide to the National Park System.* Her columns have appeared in *The Detroit News*; her poetry, short stories, articles, in hundreds of magazines such as *Iris, English Journal.*

SANDRA SUNQUIST STANTON is a Nationally Certified and Licensed Professional Counselor, and Past President of the Wisconsin School Counselor Association. She published curricula for teaching developmental classes in K-12 schools, articles in professional journal such as *ASCA School Counselor, Wisconsin School Counselor.*

SAMUEL TOTTEN is Professor of Curriculum and Instruction at the University of Arkansas, Fayetteville, director of Northwest Arkansas Writing Project, an affiliate of the National Writing Project. Among his books are: *Researching and Teaching Social Issues: The Personal Stories and Pedagogical Efforts of Professors of Education; Teaching About Genocide.*

RICHARD WEISSMAN is Associate Professor Emeritus in Music & Entertainment Business Studies, University of Colorado at Denver, and is an adjunct professor at the University of Oregon and the University of Denver. He has written 12 published books about music such as *Music Making In America, The Music Business: Career Opportunities & Self Defense.*